# Inspired

## A 21st-Century Twist on 19th-Century Favorites



# DAWN HEESE

# *Inspired*

## A 21ST-CENTURY TWIST ON 19TH-CENTURY FAVORITES
By Dawn Heese

**Editor:** Kimber Mitchell
**Designer:** Bob Deck
**Photography:** Aaron T. Leimkuehler
**Illustration:** Eric Sears
**Technical Editor:** Nan Doljac
**Production assistance:** Jo Ann Groves

**Published by:**
Kansas City Star Books
1729 Grand Blvd.
Kansas City, Missouri, USA 64108



First edition, first printing
ISBN: 978-1-61169-058-3

Library of Congress Control Number: 2012942881

Printed in the United States of America
By Walsworth Publishing Co., Marceline, MO

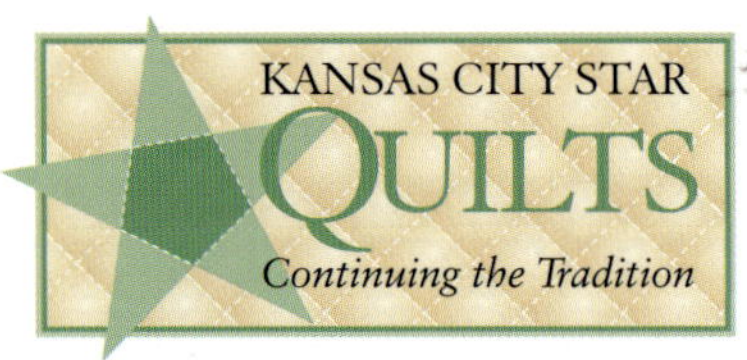

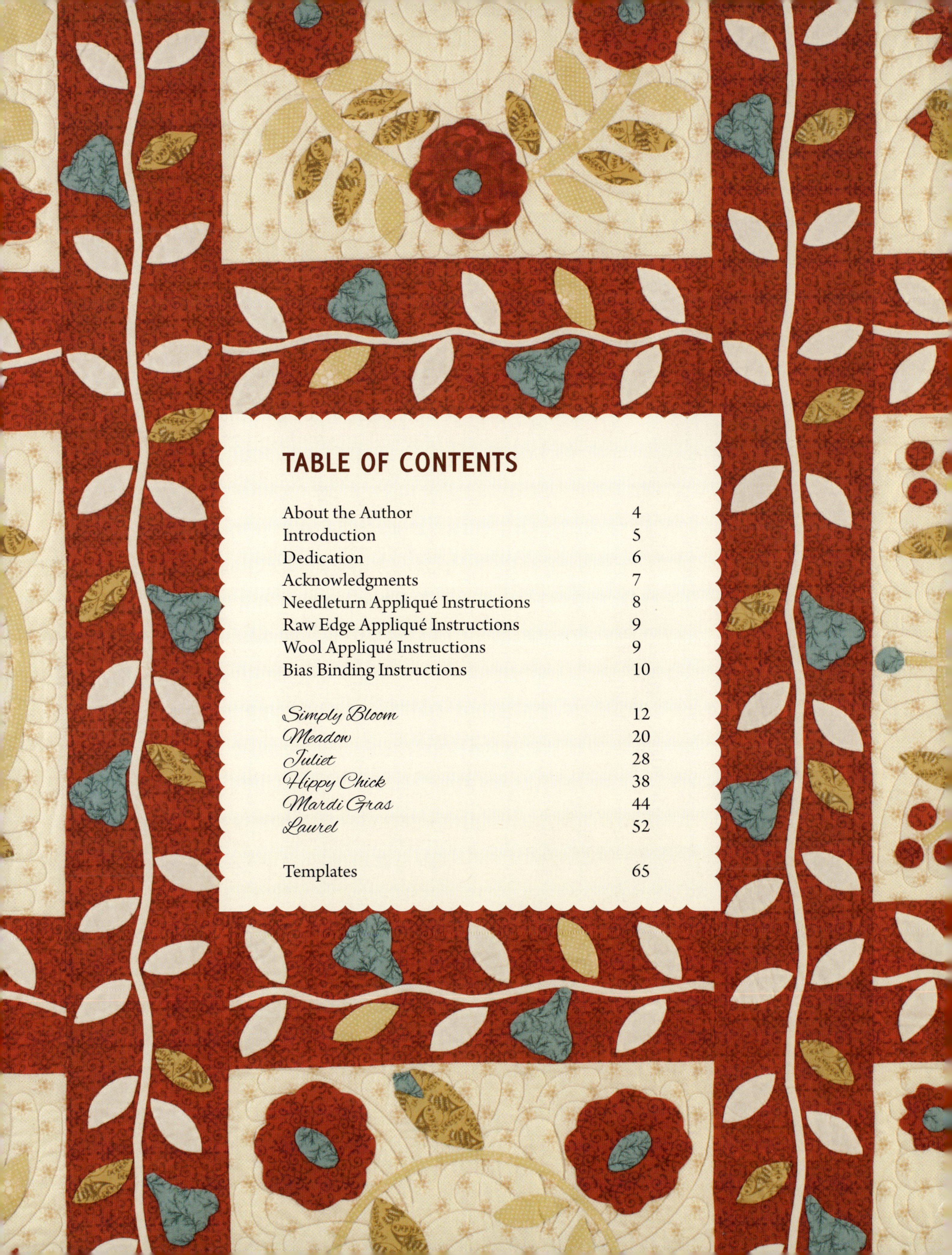

# TABLE OF CONTENTS

## ABOUT THE AUTHOR

Dawn Heese is a third-generation quilter and an avid cross stitcher. Inspired by a quilt pattern in a magazine, she bought her first rotary cutter and mat in 1999 and hasn't stopped quilting since. She particularly enjoys needleturn appliqué and hand quilting. Her love of traditional designs stems from fond childhood memories of being surrounded by quilts.

Dawn lives in Columbia, Missouri, with her two teenage sons and works as a hairstylist. She is a member of the Boonslick Trail Quilters Guild as well as several sewing groups. Dawn teaches at quilt shops and guilds nationwide. She has her own pattern company, Linen Closet Designs, and her designs have been featured in national magazines. This is her fourth book with Kansas City Star Quilts. Follow Dawn's quilting adventures and get free quilt patterns at her blog, dawnheesequilts.blogspot.com.

# INTRODUCTION

When I travel to speak and teach about my quilt designs, the one question I am asked most often is "Where do you find your inspiration?" The answer is almost always vintage/antique textiles and quilts. I love old quilts. Each quilt has a story to tell and its own personality. It may be serious and formal or quirky and casual. After all, quilts are as varied as their makers.

I don't make reproduction quilts but there is generally an element of antique quilts in each of my designs. Many of my quilts have been inspired by 19th-century examples. I am particularly drawn to the 1840-1865 era. I do a lot of appliqué designs, and I love the red and green quilts from that period. I am also drawn to the brown and muddy shades of the Civil War period. The quilts in this book are all designs that are easily recognized as 19th-century designs, but I have given each my own unique twist. Sometimes the colors of an antique quilt may inspire my design, or I may refresh a well-known design from the past with colors and fabrics that speak of the 21st century. I may even keep the traditional colors of an antique quilt design but use modern methods of construction to update it for today's quilters. My quilts reflect the way today's quilters live. Once upon a time, quilts were made strictly to keep warm for beds or cribs. Today, we make our quilts in many sizes and use them as much for décor as warmth.

I hope you will be inspired to make one or more of the six quilts in this book. So join me in uniting past with present as you stitch them!

*Dawn*

DEDICATION

This book is
dedicated to all
the quilters who
came before me
and to their legacy
of inspiration.

# ACKNOWLEDGMENTS

An author is only as good as the team who helps bring her book alive. Creating a book is not a one-person endeavor; there are many hardworking people involved. I want to thank and acknowledge the following individuals for their important role in making this book happen:

Doug Weaver and Diane McLendon gave me my start in book publishing and continue to allow me artistic freedom to produce books that are truly me.

My editor, Kimber Mitchell, has been with me on all four of my books. She cleans up my writing and always finds the words that I can't. I can't imagine writing a book without her.

Bob Deck, my graphic designer, has also been with me for all my books. Thanks, Bob, for all you do.

Aaron Leimkuehler, my photographer, takes the gorgeous photos that make Kansas City Star quilt books stand out.

Jo Ann Groves does all the behind-the-scenes technical work to the photos to make them look their best.

Nan Doljac, my technical editor, double- and triple-checks my calculations to make sure I don't steer you wrong.

Eric Sears, illustrator extraordinaire, creates all the wonderful diagrams to guide you through the quiltmaking process.

Thanks also to the folks at The Gentle Art for providing the Simply Wool thread for my stitching.

A special thanks to Tammy Bush and Christy Gray for their beautiful quilting. They worked with my impossible deadlines and saved the day!

A special thanks also goes to Kristie and Ryan Williams, who opened their beautiful home to us for the photo shoot. It is their home you see in all the setting shots in this book.

# NEEDLETURN APPLIQUÉ

There are many ways to appliqué. My way is not the "right way," just the method that works best for me. I love to appliqué by hand but I don't like to spend my time doing prep work. I prefer to get right to the stitching! Since I carry my appliqué with me practically everywhere I go, my method requires very few supplies so I don't have to tote a ton of them along. Here are some needleturn appliqué basics:

1. Trace the template shapes on the dull side of a piece of freezer paper. Do not add a seam allowance to the templates. Cut out the templates on the drawn line. The freezer paper will adhere to the fabric many times. If you need four of the same leaf, for example, you need only cut one paper template and reuse it.

2. When I cut my background fabric squares to size, I seal their edges with Fray Check to prevent raveling and distortion. This prevents me from having to cut the block, then resize it after stitching it.

3. Fold your background fabric square in half vertically and horizontally, finger-pressing the folds. Then fold on both diagonals and finger-press. These fold lines will serve as a guide for placing the appliqué shapes on the background fabric.

4. Iron the paper templates, shiny side down, to the right side of the appliqué fabrics. Using a chalk pencil (I prefer Generals brand as they mark easily), trace around the template. Make sure the line is clearly visible as this will be your turn line. Add a ⅛" – ¼" seam allowance around the template, then cut it out.

5. Pin or baste the appliqué shape in place on the background fabric square (I like Clover appliqué pins as they have a thick shaft that keeps them from backing out of the piece. Their oval heads are also less likely to snag your thread).

6. Sew the appliqué shapes in the order that they are layered, starting with the bottom pieces. Use the tip of your needle or a toothpick to turn under your seam allowance.

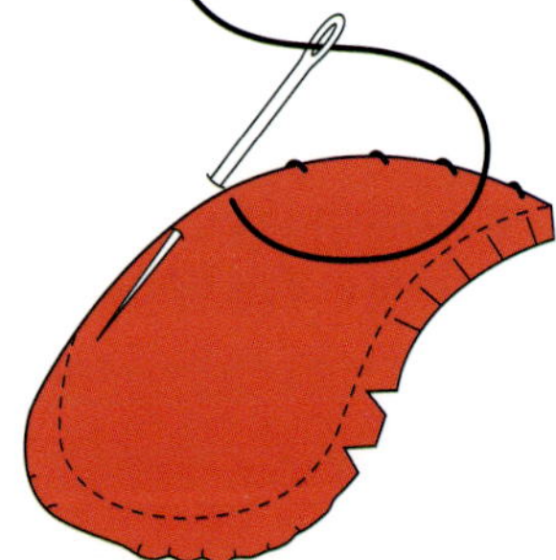

7. When appliquéing, I recommend using YLI 100-weight silk thread in a neutral color because it sinks into the fabric and practically disappears. Using a neutral color also eliminates the worry about matching all the pieces with coordinating thread colors. YLI #242 and #235 will match any color you need.

# RAW-EDGE APPLIQUÉ

1.  Following the manufacturer's instructions, fuse the web to a piece of fabric about the size of half a fat quarter at a time. I like to use Steam-a-Seam Lite.

2.  Trace the appliqué shapes onto the wrong side of the fused fabric. Then cut them out and remove the paper backing.

3.  Lay out all the pieces for each block on the background squares before fusing them in place.

4.  Stitch the appliqué pieces to the background squares with a straight stitch right along the edge of the shapes with a matching thread, getting as close to the edge as possible. This makes the stitches less obvious and doesn't leave a wide seam allowance to curl up.

# WOOL APPLIQUÉ

I love the texture of wool appliqué. In addition to working with wool on wool, I like to mix wool with cotton backgrounds. One of the benefits of using wool is that it does not unravel, which means you do not have to turn under its edges or add a seam allowance. The process is so fast and rewarding that you will be soon be addicted to wool appliqué! Here's how to do it:

1.  Trace your templates onto the dull side of a piece of freezer paper. Cut them out on the drawn line.

2.  Iron the shiny side of the templates to the wool and cut them out without a seam allowance.

3.  Pin or baste the wool in place on your fabric background square.

4.  To stitch, I like to use two strands of embroidery floss that will match my appliqué piece. I prefer Weeks Dye Works hand-dyed floss because it is variegated and usually best matches the hand-dyed wools I like to use. I am also in love with hand-dyed Simply Wool thread from The Gentle Art, Inc., and use one strand of it to appliqué. To secure the appliqué pieces, I take a $\frac{1}{8}$" stitch perpendicular to the edge of the appliqué piece. This small, simple stitch will barely be noticeable.

# BIAS BINDING INSTRUCTIONS

Bias binding is used for curved borders, such as the scalloped one featured in my Laurel quilt on page 52, because bias strips have a natural stretch that allows you to easily follow the curves of the quilt. Here is a fast and easy method for cutting bias strips:

1. Fold your fabric in half diagonally to form a 45-degree angle.

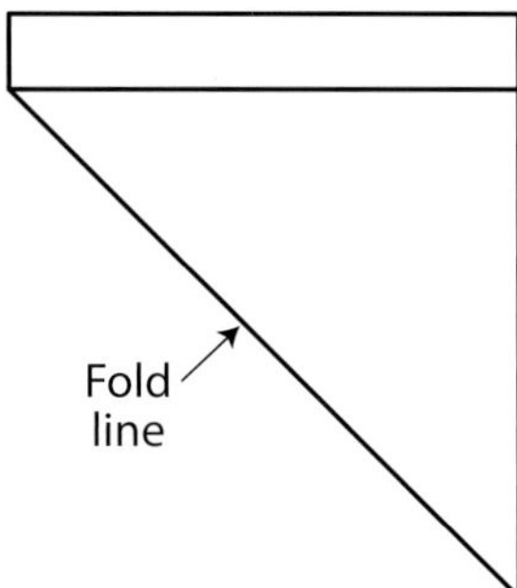


2. Fold the fabric a second time by bringing the top left corner down to the bottom right corner, creating a second 45-degree angle. Smooth the fabric.

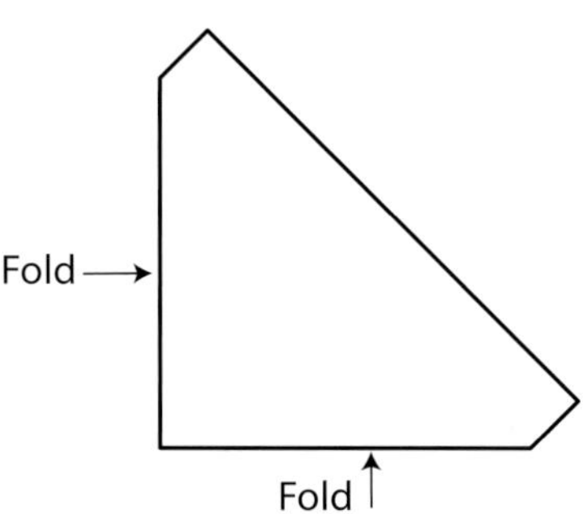


3. Cut off the fold on the left side of the triangle.

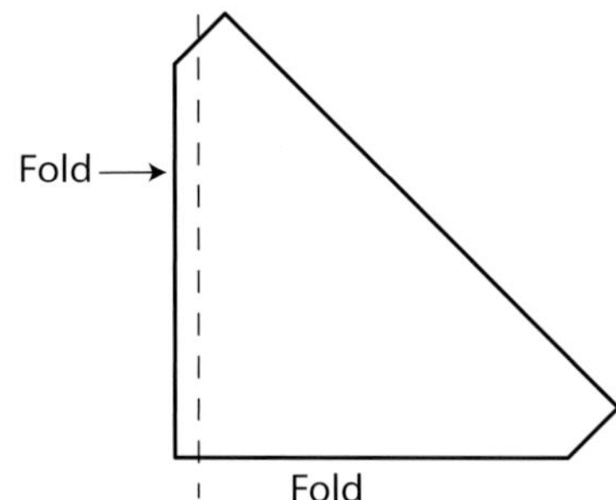


4. Cut your strips whatever width you prefer. Typically, I cut either a 2"- or 2 ¼"-wide strip for a durable double-fold binding.

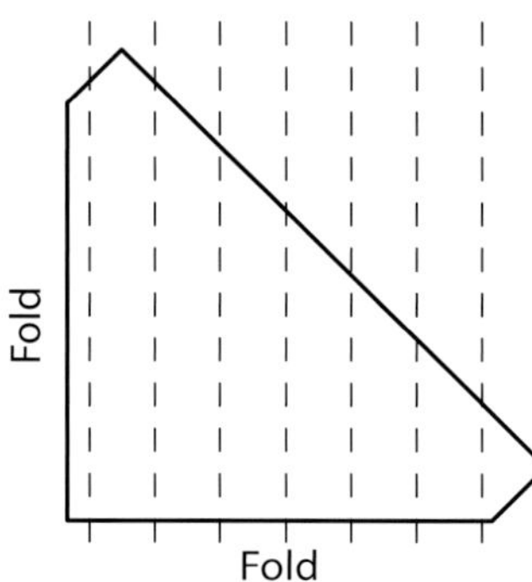


5. Join the strips on the diagonal.

Welcome
Projects

Simply Bloom
Hand appliquéd and hand quilted by Dawn Heese

FINISHED QUILT: 54" x 54"
FINISHED BLOCK: 18" x 18"

## COTTON

- ○ 2 ¾ yards tan stripe for block and border backgrounds and sashing
- ○ Fat eighth pink stripe for appliqué diamonds
- ○ ½ yard brown/green print for sashing

## WOOL

- ○ Fat sixteenth gold for red flower centers and lower buds
- ○ Fat eighth off white for flower centers, urn accents, and border flower centers
- ○ Fat eighth pink for lower bud cups
- ○ Fat eighth red for upper center and lower blooms
- ○ Fat quarter different red than above for flower petals and border blooms
- ○ Fat eighth blue for border flowers
- ○ Fat quarter different blue than above for urns
- ○ Fat quarter gold/green for leaves
- ○ 2 fat quarters brown/green for block and border leaves and stems
- ○ Fat quarter purple for side blooms and border leaves

*Cutting Instructions*

**From tan stripe background print, cut:**
- 4—18 ½" squares for block backgrounds. Then seal the edges with Fray Check to prevent raveling and distortion
- 54—2 ⅞" squares for sashing
- 9—2 ½" squares for sashing
- 6—6 ½" strips the width of fabric for borders

**From brown/green print, cut:**
- 54—2 ⅞" squares for sashing

**From pink stripe, gold wool, off white wool, pink wool, two red wools, two blue wools, gold/green wool, brown/green wool, and purple wool, cut:**
- Templates on pages 65—67 the number of times noted

## APPLIQUÉ BLOCKS

Referring to the following photo for placement, appliqué the shapes onto the prepared background squares. The stems are made from 1/4"-wide strips cut on the bias. Referring to the diagram at right, embroider small stems on the leaves with a stem stitch and two strands of floss. Make a total of four appliquéd blocks.

STEM STITCH

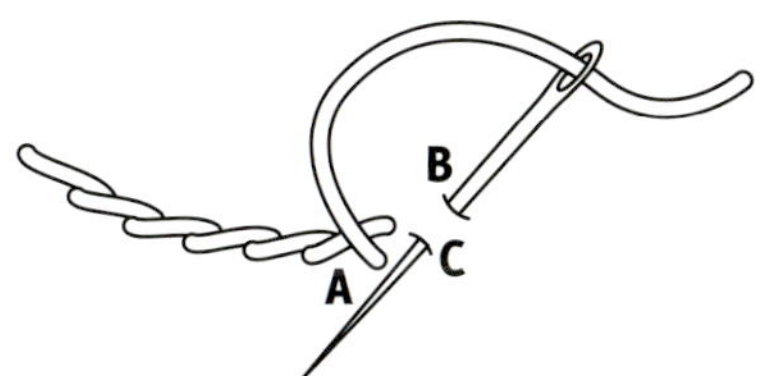

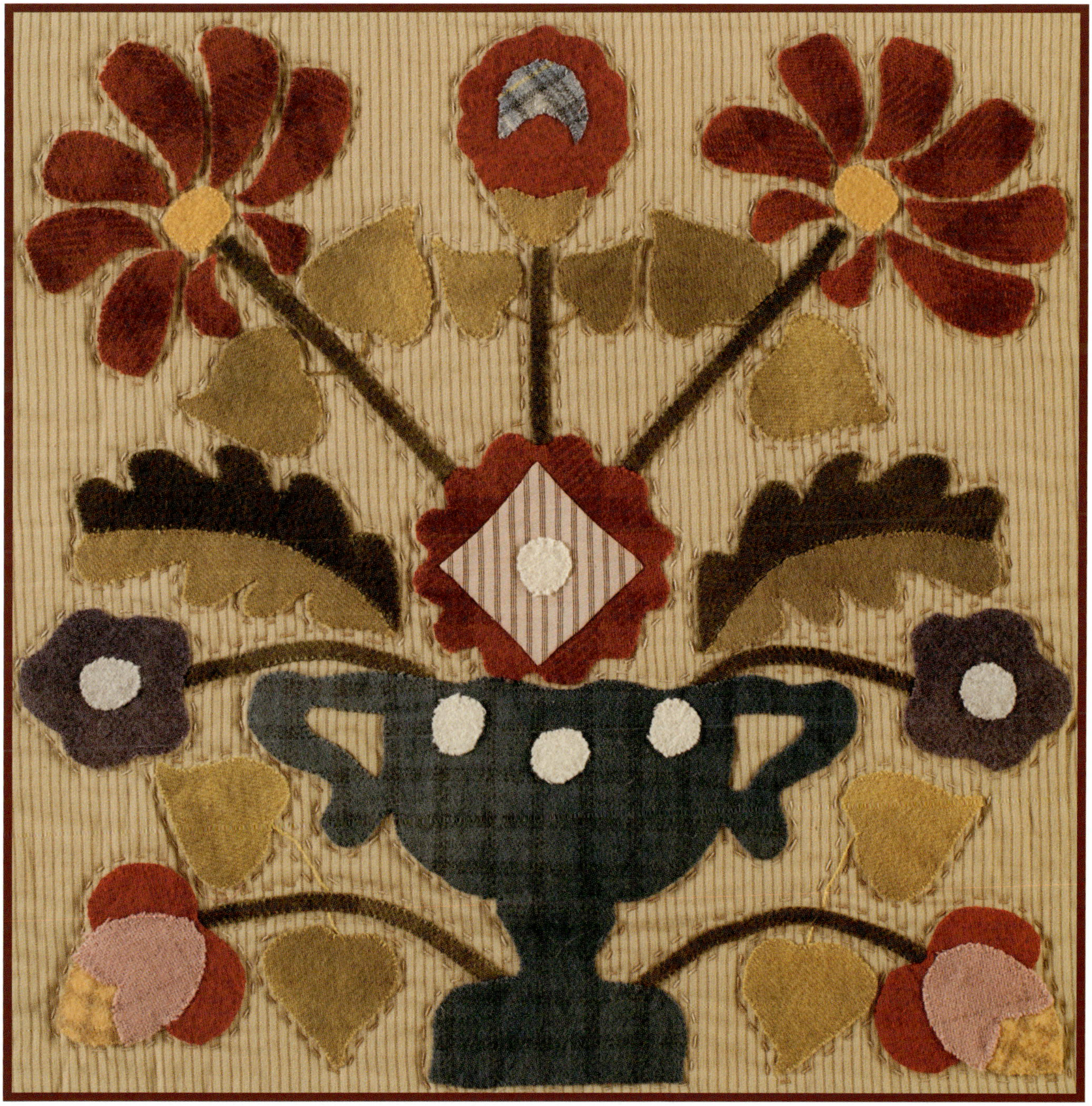

## SASHING

1. On the wrong side of the 54—2 ⅞" tan stripe squares, draw a diagonal line from corner to corner. With right sides together, layer the marked tan stripe squares on the brown/green squares. Sew a ¼" seam allowance on each side of the drawn line.

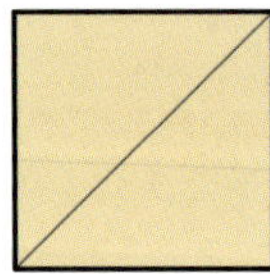 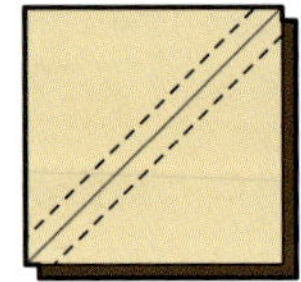

2. Cut apart on the line and press open to yield two half-square triangle units. Repeat to make a total of 108 half-square triangle units.

3. Sew together nine half-square triangle units to create a sashing strip. Repeat to make a total of 12 strips.

4. Referring to the following diagram, sew together two sashing strips and 3—2 ½" tan stripe squares to create a sashing row. Repeat to make a total of three of these sashing rows.

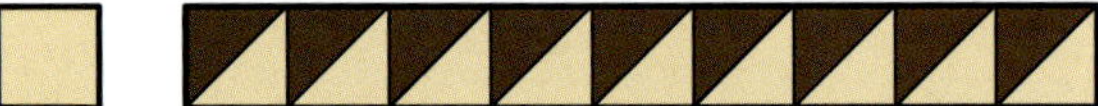  

## TOP AND BOTTOM BORDERS

Join 6 ½" x WOF (width of fabric) strips, then cut to measure 6 ½" x 42 ½". Repeat to make a total of two border strips. Seal the edges with Fray Check. Referring to the photo below for placement, appliqué the flowers, leaves, and vines to the border strips. The stems are made from ¼"-wide strips cut on the bias.

## SIDE BORDERS

Join the remaining 6 ½" x WOF strips, then cut to measure 6 ½" x 54 ½". Repeat to make a total of two side border strips. Seal the edges with Fray Check. Referring to the photo below for placement, appliqué the shapes to the border strips. The stems are made from ¼"-wide strips cut on the bias.

1.  Referring to the following diagram, sew together two finished appliqué blocks with three sashing strips from step 3 in the Sashing section. Repeat to make a total of two of these rows.

2.  Join the three sashing rows from step 4 in the Sashing section with the two block rows from the previous step to create the quilt center.

3.  Referring to the quilt assembly diagram on page 19, sew the finished appliquéd top and bottom borders to the quilt center.

4.  Referring to the quilt assembly diagram, sew the finished appliquéd side borders to the quilt center.

5.  Sandwich the quilt top, batting, and backing; baste. Quilt as desired, then bind. I quilted mine with the Big Stitch method (a form of hand quilting done with a larger stitch and perle cotton), using Valdani hand-dyed No. 8 perle cotton. The blocks, sashing, and borders are quilted in the ditch. I then outlined about ¼" around the appliqué in all the blocks and borders.

QUILT ASSEMBLY DIAGRAM

Meadow
Machine pieced by Dawn Heese
Machine quilted by Christy Gray of Katydid Design Studio

*Known as a bar or strip style*, this quilt has a decidedly 1800s flavor. Even with the most modern prints, it retains some of its 19th-century character. In the 1800s, it was common to use a sampling of simply pieced blocks for this type of quilt. You can transform basic blocks from ordinary to extraordinary by setting them on point and adding wide sashing between the vertical rows. This setting is also a good option for using a few odd orphan blocks from other projects. I made my quilt with recently released floral prints. I think these romantic prints add softness to the geometric design.

FINISHED QUILT: 54" X 67 ½"
FINISHED BLOCKS: 6" X 6"

## Fabric Requirements

- 6 fat quarters total of assorted brown prints for setting and corner triangles in vertical rows
- 3 fat quarters total of assorted red prints for Nine-Patch and Four-Patch blocks
- 3 fat quarters total of light cream floral for Nine-Patch, Four-Patch, and Churn Dash blocks
- Fat quarter total of assorted blue prints for Churn Dash blocks
- 1 ½ yards darker cream floral for sashing

## Cutting Instructions

**From assorted brown prints, cut:**
- 12—9 ¾" squares for setting triangles. Then cut squares on the diagonal twice to yield a total of 48 setting triangles
- 8—5 ⅛" squares for corner triangles. Then cut squares on the diagonal once to yield a total of 16 corner triangles

**From assorted red prints, cut:**
- 60—2 ½" squares for Nine-Patch blocks
- 26—3 ½" squares for Four-Patch blocks

**From light cream floral, cut:**
- 51—2 ½" squares for Nine-Patch blocks and Churn-Dash blocks
- 26—3 ½" squares for Four-Patch blocks
- 12—1 ½" x 2 ½" rectangles for Churn Dash blocks
- 6—2 ⅞" squares for Churn Dash blocks

**From assorted blue prints, cut:**
- 12—1 ½" x 2 ½" rectangles for Churn Dash blocks
- 6—2 ⅞" squares for Churn Dash blocks

**From darker cream floral print, cut:**
- 11—4 ½" strips the width of fabric for sashing and border

*Sewing Instructions*

## NINE-PATCH BLOCKS

1. Sew together two 2 ½" red print squares and a 2 ½" light cream print square to create a block row. Repeat to make a total of 24 rows.

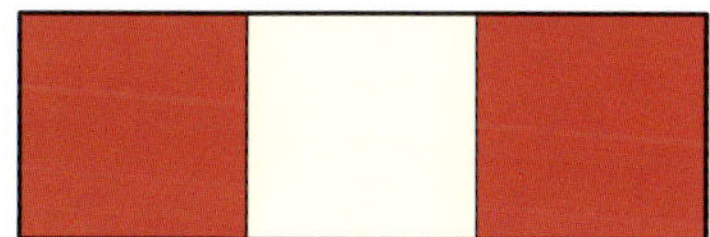

2. Sew together two 2 ½" light cream print squares and a 2 ½" red print square to create a block row. Repeat to make a total of 12 rows.

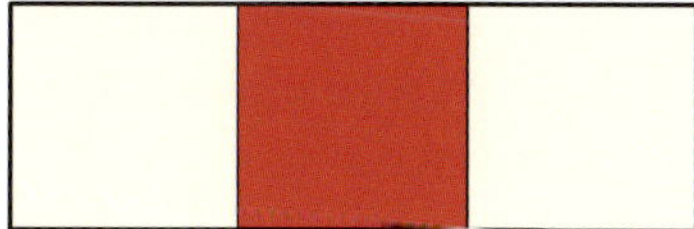

3. Join the rows from steps 1 and 2 to create a Nine-Patch block, which should measure 6" finished. Repeat to make a total of 12 Nine-Patch blocks.

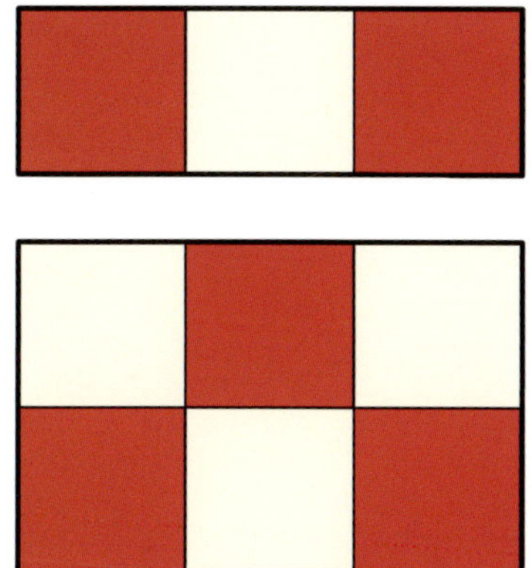

## FOUR-PATCH BLOCKS

1. Sew together a 3 ½" red print square and 3 ½" light cream print square. Repeat to make a total of 26 of these units.

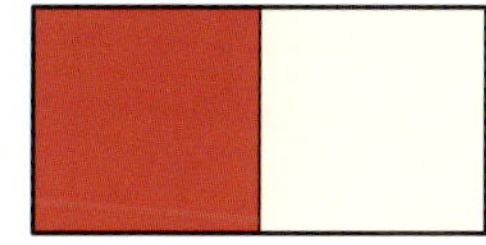

2. Join two units from step 1 to create a Four-Patch block, which should measure 6" finished. Repeat to make a total of 13 Four-Patch blocks.

## CHURN DASH BLOCKS

1. On the wrong side of the six 2 ⅞" light cream squares, draw a diagonal line from corner to corner. With right sides together, layer the marked cream squares with the 2 ⅞" blue squares. Sew a ¼" seam allowance on both sides of the drawn line.

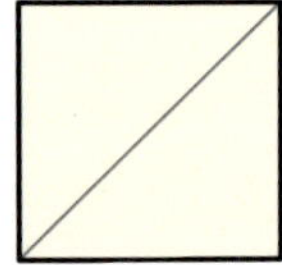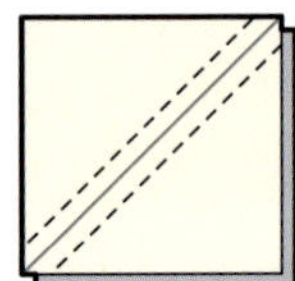

2. Cut apart on the drawn line and press open to create half-square triangle units. Repeat to make a total of 12 half-square triangle units.

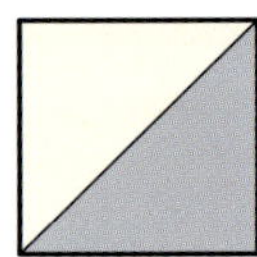

3. Sew together one 1 ½" x 2 ½" light cream rectangle and one 1 ½" x 2 ½" blue print rectangle. Repeat to make a total of 12 of these units.

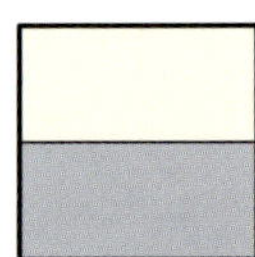

4. Sew together four half-square triangle units from step 2, four units from step 3, and one 2 ½" cream print square to create a Churn Dash block. Repeat to make a total of three Churn Dash blocks.

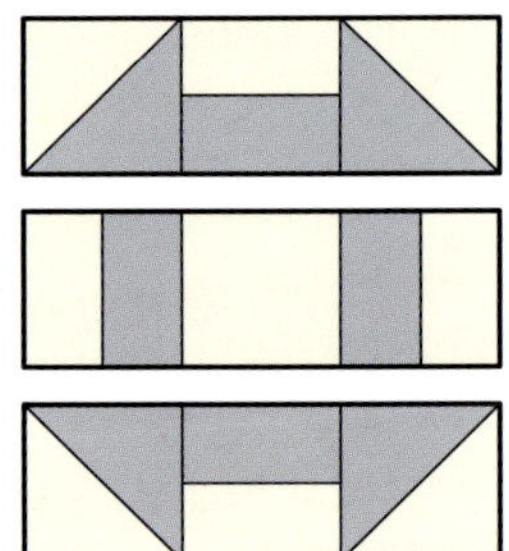

## PIECED VERTICAL ROWS

This quilt consists of four vertical rows comprised of seven pieced blocks each, then set together diagonally with setting and corner triangles.

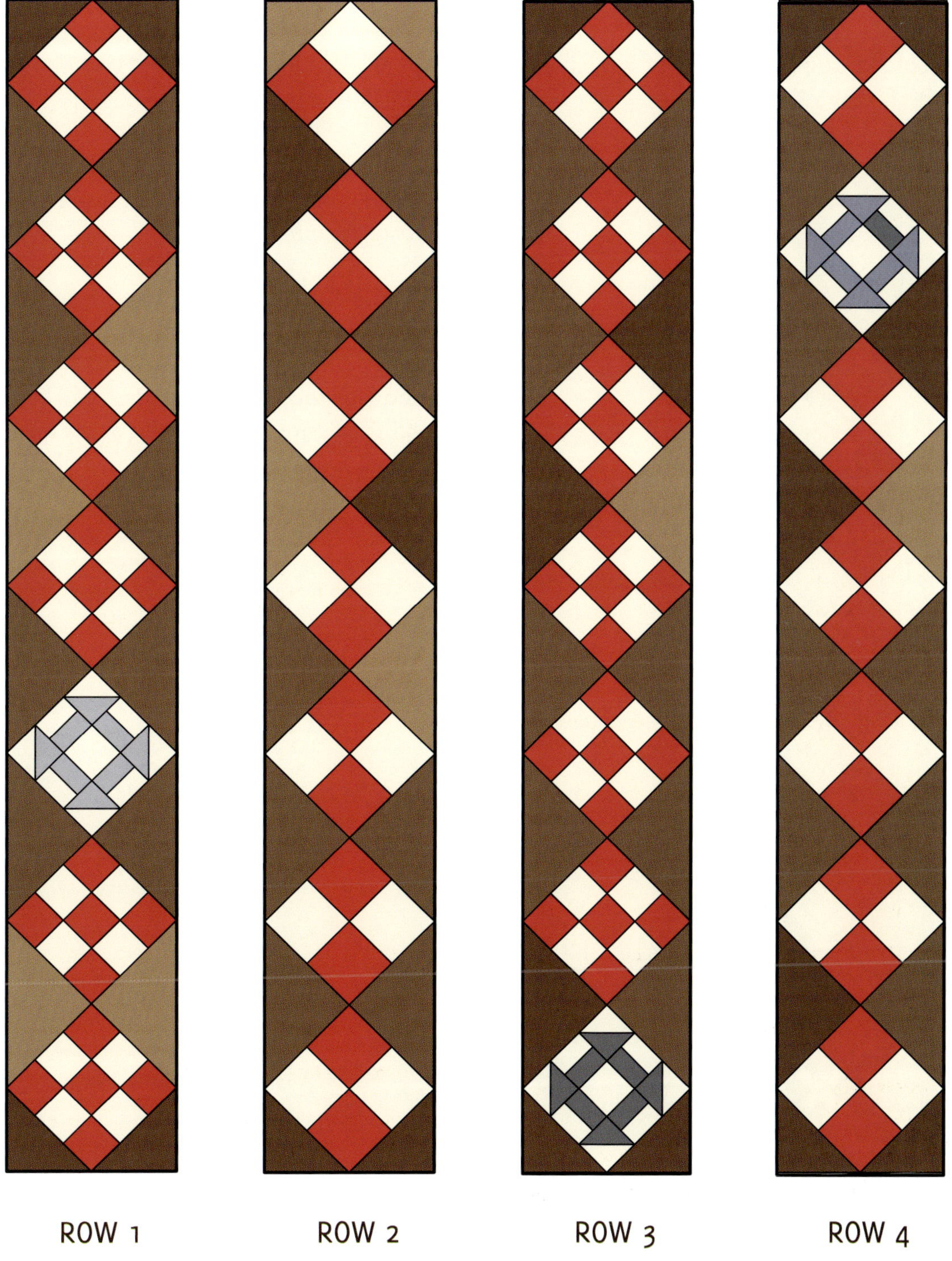

ROW 1    ROW 2    ROW 3    ROW 4

Referring to the following diagram, assemble each vertical row individually with 12 setting triangles and four corner triangles. As you assemble them, pay close attention to the placement of blocks. Each row varies in terms of its blocks. This diagram illustrates the first vertical row only, but the remaining three rows are pieced in the same fashion. You should have a total of four rows comprised of seven pieced blocks each.

## QUILT ASSEMBLY

1. Referring to the quilt assembly diagram on page 27, join the 4 ½" x WOF strips to measure 4 ½" x 59 ½". Repeat to make a total of five strips.

2. Referring to the quilt assembly diagram, join the 4 ½" x WOF strips to measure 4 ½" x 54 ½". Repeat to make a total of two strips.

3. Referring to the quilt assembly diagram, join the four pieced vertical strips with the five 4 ½" x 59 ½" strips to create the quilt center.

4. Sew the 4 ½" x 54 ½" strips to the top and bottom of the quilt center.

5. Sandwich the quilt top, batting, and backing; baste. Quilt as desired, then bind. For my quilt, Christy quilted an all-over, old-fashioned floral design in a very fine thread.

QUILT ASSEMBLY DIAGRAM

# Juliet

Hand appliquéd and hand quilted by Dawn Heese

The Rose Tree block is traditionally made with red and green appliqué on a muslin background. I tend to decorate my home with primitive touches, so I gave this throw-size quilt a prim feel, which is a real departure from 19th-century versions.

To create a primitive look, I opted for darker colors with a grayed-down appearance. As a result, my appliqué shapes have a folk art feel even though they're clearly a Rose Tree design.

FINISHED QUILT: 51 ¼" X 51 ¼"
FINISHED BLOCK: 15" X 15"

# Fabric Requirements

- ○ 2 yards tan print for block backgrounds, setting triangles, and corner triangles
- ○ ½ yard total of assorted red prints for appliqué and cornerstones
- ○ ¾ yard total of assorted green prints for leaves and stems
- ○ ⅞ yard pink print for flower accents, flower base, and inner border
- ○ ½ yard red print for outer border

# Cutting Instructions

**From tan print, cut:**
- 5—15 ½" squares for appliqué blocks. Then seal the edges with Fray Check
- 1—22 ½" square for setting triangles. Then cut square twice diagonally from corner to yield four setting triangles

- 2—11 ½" squares for corner triangles. Then cut squares once diagonally from corner to corner to yield four corner triangles

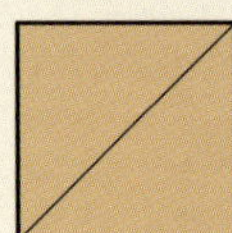

**From pink print, cut:**
- 16—1 ½" x 15 ½" strips for sashing
- 6—1 ½" strips the width of fabric for inner border

**From red print, cut:**
- 4—1 ½" squares for cornerstones
- 2—2 ⅝" squares for cornerstone triangles. Then cut squares twice diagonally from corner to corner to yield 8 cornerstone triangles

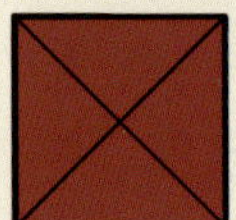

**From assorted red prints, assorted green prints, and pink print, cut:**
- Templates on page 68 the number of times noted

**From red border print, cut:**
- 6—2 ½" strips the width of fabric for outer border

## APPLIQUÉ BLOCKS

1. Apply Fray Check to the edges of the 15 ½" tan print
   background squares to prevent raveling
   and distortion.

2. Referring to the templates on page 68 and the photo
   below, cut out appliqué shapes and appliqué them to
   the background squares.

3. Make the stems using a ½" bias tape maker.

1. Sew a red cornerstone triangle to each end of a pink print sashing strip. Then sew the completed strip to a corner triangle.

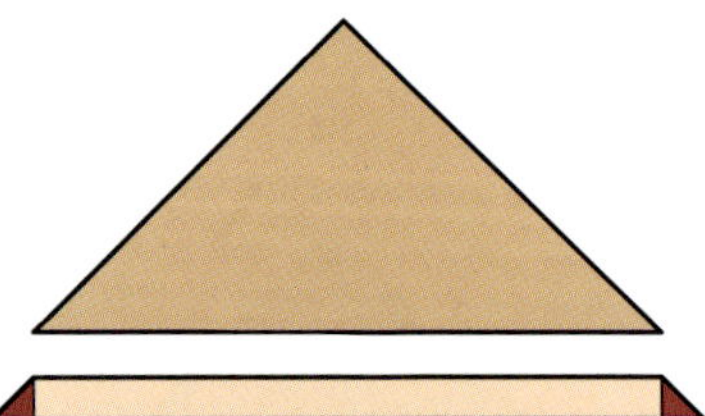

2. Referring to the following diagram, sew together two setting triangles, two pink print sashing strips, and one appliqué block.

3. Sew the unit from step 1 to the top of the unit from the previous step.

4. Referring to the following diagram for placement, sew together two red print cornerstone triangles, two red print cornerstone squares, and three pink print sashing strips to create a sashing row. Repeat to make a total of two sashing rows.

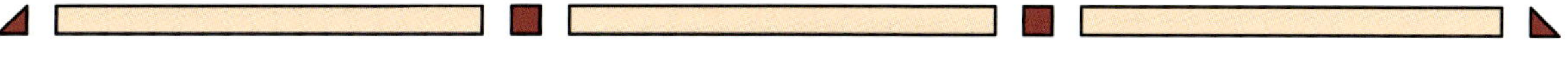

5. Join one of the sashing strips from the previous step to the unit from step 3.

6. Referring to the following diagram for placement, sew together two corner triangles, three appliqué blocks, and four pink sashing strips. This creates the center row of the quilt.

**7.** Join the unit from step 6 to the unit from step 5 and the remaining sashing row from step 4.

**8.** Referring to the following diagram for placement, sew together two setting triangles, one appliqué block, and two pink print sashing strips. Then join this unit to the unit from step 7.

9. Sew a red cornerstone triangle to each end of a pink print sashing strip. Then sew the completed strip to a corner triangle.

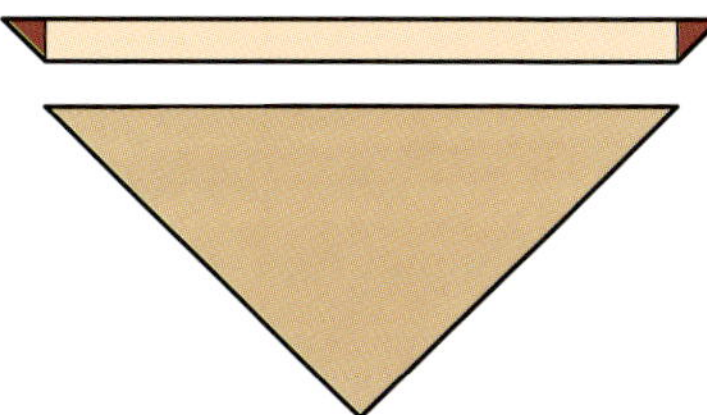

10. Join the unit from step 9 to the unit from step 8 to complete the quilt center.

## INNER BORDER

1. Join the 1 ½" x WOF pink border strips to create 2—1 ½" x 45 ¾" border strips. Referring to the quilt assembly diagram on page 37, sew the two border strips to the sides of the quilt center.

2. Join the remaining 1 ½" x WOF pink border strips to create 2—1 ½" x 47 ¾" border strips. Referring to the quilt assembly diagram, sew the two border strips to the top and bottom of the quilt center.

## OUTER BORDER

1. Join the 2 ½" x WOF red border strips to create 2—2 ½" x 47 ¾" border strips. Referring to the quilt assembly diagram, sew the two border strips to the sides of the quilt top.

2. Join the remaining 2 ½" x WOF red border strips to create 2—2 ½" x 51 ¾" border strips. Referring to the quilt assembly diagram, sew the two border strips to the top and bottom of the top.

3. Sandwich the quilt top, batting, and backing; baste. Quilt as desired, then bind. I used the Big Stitch method (a form of hand quilting done with a larger stitch and perle cotton), using hand-dyed Valdani perle cotton. I stitched-in-the-ditch around all the blocks and sashing, then outline-quilted around all the appliqué and bloom accents. A single line was stitched down the center of the outer border.

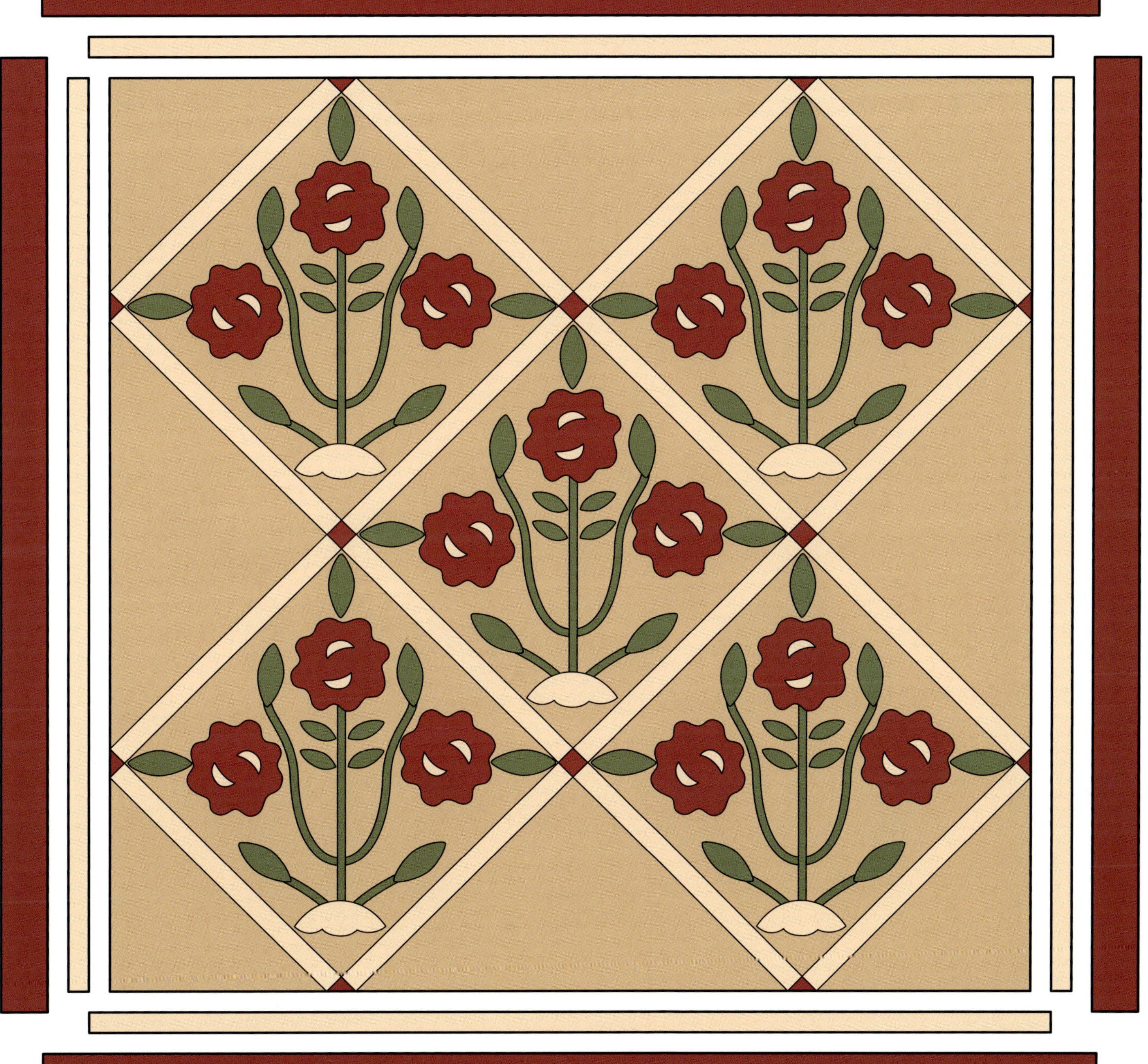

QUILT ASSEMBLY DIAGRAM

Hippy Chick
Machine pieced and hand appliquéd by Dawn Heese
Machine quilted by Christy Gray of Katydid Design Studio

*The featured block* in this quilt is known as Snowball, and the color placement of the blocks creates a secondary hourglass design known as Broken Dishes. Nineteenth-century quilts in this design were often made with two colors. The positive-negative color scheme adds movement. If you look closely, you will see stars flickering among the Snowball blocks! Thanks to updated techniques, you can make this quilt a lot faster than quilters of the past. I made my Snowball blocks by sewing squares onto larger squares, then flipping them open to form a triangle in the corners. I stepped out of my box and into the 21st century with my fabric choices, which are truly modern in feel. To give the quilt even more personality, I added a touch of appliqué. The pictured quilt is throw-size but I've also included instructions for making a twin-size version. The latter would look great on a girl's bed.

FINISHED THROW-SIZE QUILT (SHOWN): 54" X 54"
FINISHED TWIN-SIZE QUILT (NOT SHOWN): 66" X 90"
FINISHED BLOCK: 6" X 6"

## *Fabric Requirements*

Yardage for alternate twin-size quilt is listed in parentheses

- 2 ⅛ yards orange print for blocks (4 ¼ yards for twin size)
- 10" x 10" different orange print than above for flower centers (⅛ yard for twin size)
- 2 ⅛ yards total of green and teal prints for blocks (4 ¼ yards for twin size)
- Fat quarter white tone-on-tone for flower petals (⅓ yard for twin size)
- ½ yard different white tone-on-tone than above for binding (⅝ yard for twin size)


## *Cutting Instructions*

Twin-size dimensions are listed in parentheses

**From orange print, cut:**
- 41—6 ½" squares (83—6 ½" squares for twin size)
- 160—2 ½" squares (328—2 ½" squares for twin size)
- 7 flower centers from template on page 69 (13 flower centers for twin size)

**From green and teal prints, cut:**
- 40—6 ½" squares (82—6 ½" squares for twin size)
- 164—2 ½" squares (332—2 ½" squares for twin size)

**From white tone-on-tone, cut:**
- 28 white petals from template on page 69 (52 petals for twin size)

## SNOWBALL BLOCKS

1. On the wrong side of the 2 ½" orange print and green/teal print squares, draw a line diagonally from corner to corner.

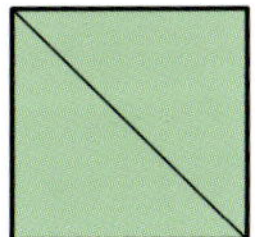 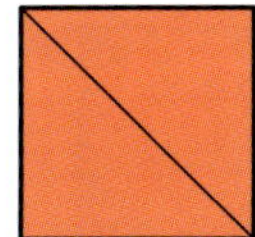

2. With right sides together, layer a 2 ½" green/teal print square on one corner of a 6 ½" orange print square. Sew on the drawn line. Press back, creating a triangle, then trim away the extra layers of fabric underneath, leaving a ¼" seam allowance.

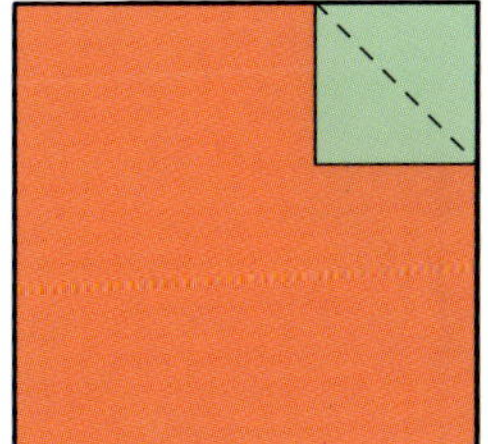 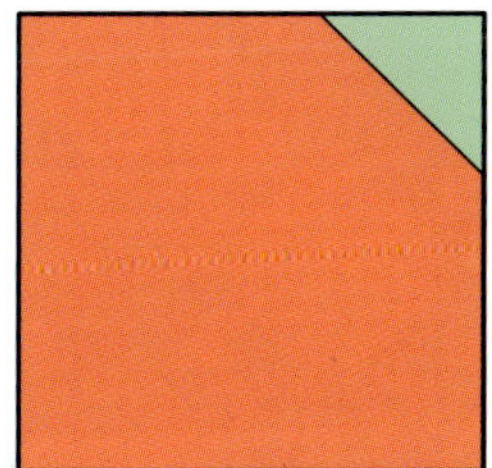

3. Repeat step 2 for the remaining three corners to create a Snowball block. Repeat this step and step 2 to make a total of 41 Snowball blocks (For the twin-size version, you will need to make 83 blocks).

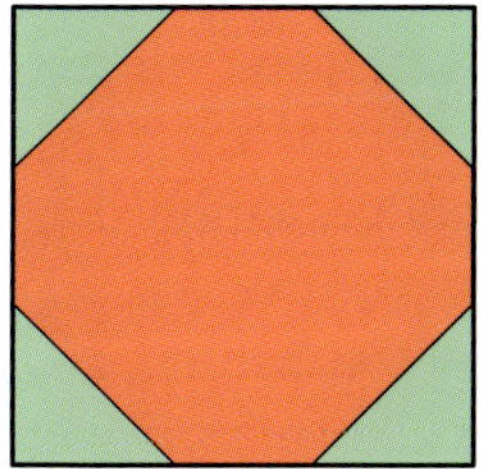

4. Repeat steps 2-3 with the 2 ½" orange print squares on the corners of the 6 ½" teal/green print squares to make a total of 40 Snowball blocks (For the twin-size version, you will need to make 82 blocks).

## APPLIQUÉ

Referring to the photo below for placement, appliqué daisy shapes to seven teal green with orange print corner triangle blocks (For the twin-size version, you will need 13 appliqué blocks).

1. Referring to the quilt assembly diagram below, assemble nine rows of nine blocks each, paying careful attention to the placement of the appliquéd blocks (For the twin-size version on page 43, you will need 15 rows of 11 blocks each).

2. Referring to the quilt assembly diagram, join the rows to create the quilt top.

3. Sandwich the quilt top, batting, and backing; baste. Quilt as desired, then bind. Christy quilted an all-over modified paisley design on my quilt. She used a super-fine thread that creates texture without competing with the busy fabrics and design. To finish off the quilt without adding borders, I bound my quilt with a white fabric that brings out the daisy appliqué.

**THROW-SIZE QUILT ASSEMBLY DIAGRAM**

TWIN-SIZE QUILT ASSEMBLY DIAGRAM

# Mardi Gras

Machine appliquéd and machine pieced by Dawn Heese
Machine quilted by Tammy Bush of
Form and Function Custom Quilting

*Known as Coxcomb and Currants,* this block design typically features red and green appliqué on a muslin background. In 19th-century versions, the blocks are often set on point, alternating with plain white setting squares. This block has so much energy that I opted for an exuberant color palette of purple, gold and green—the colors of Mardi Gras—for my wall hanging. I chose to spotlight four oversized blocks with no sashing. I took a modern approach to the appliqué, using a lightweight fusible web and raw-edge technique. A checkerboard border adds a final flourish as well as a sense of movement to the overall design.

FINISHED QUILT: 50" X 50"
FINISHED BLOCK: 20" X 20"

## Fabric Requirements

- 1 ⅔ yards light cream print for appliqué backgrounds and checkerboard border
- 1 ¼ yard green print for coxcombs and stems
- 1 ⅛ yard purple print for berries, checkerboard border, petals, buds and outer border
- ½ yard gold print for berries, checkerboard border, and flower centers

## Cutting Instructions

**From light cream print, cut:**
- 4—20 ½" squares for appliqué backgrounds. Then seal the edges with Fray Check
- 6—2 ½" strips the width of fabric for checkerboard border

**From gold print, cut:**
- 3—2 ½" strips the width of fabric for checkerboard border

**From purple print, cut:**
- 3—2 ½" strips the width of fabric for checkerboard border
- 6—1 ½" strips the width of fabric for outer border

**From gold print, purple print, and green print, cut:**
- Templates on page 70 the number of times noted

## APPLIQUÉ BLOCKS

Referring to the photo below and templates on page
70, appliqué the shapes to the background square.
Make the stems using a ½" bias tape maker. Repeat to
make a total of four blocks.

## CHECKERBOARD BORDER

1. Sew together a 2 ½" x WOF gold print strip and a 2 ½" x WOF cream print strip. Press the seam toward the gold print strip. Repeat to make a total of three of these strips.

2. Cut the strips from step 1 into 46—2 ½"-wide units.

3. Sew together a 2 ½" x WOF purple print strip and a 2 ½" x WOF cream print strip. Press the seam toward the purple print strip. Repeat to make a total of three of these strips.

4. Cut the strips from step 3 into 42—2 ½" wide units.

5. Sew one unit from step 2 to one unit from step 4 to make a Four-Patch unit. Repeat to make a total of 42 Four-Patch units.

6. Join the remaining units to make two gold/cream print Four-Patch units.

7. Join 11 gold/purple Four-Patch units and one gold Four-Patch unit to create a top border strip. Repeat to make a bottom border strip. Set it aside for now.

8. Join 10 Four-Patch units to create a side border strip. Repeat to make a second border strip. Set it aside for now.

1. Sew together the four appliqué blocks.

2. Referring to the quilt assembly diagram on page 51, sew the two checkerboard border strips created in step 8 of the Checkerboard Border section to the sides of the quilt center.

3. Referring to the quilt assembly diagram, sew the two checkerboard border strips created in step 7 of the Checkerboard Border section to the top and bottom of the quilt top.

4. Join the purple 1 ½" x WOF strips to create a 1 ½" x 48 ½" border strip. Repeat to make a total of two strips. Referring to the quilt assembly diagram, sew the two strips to the sides of the quilt top.

5. Join the purple 1 ½" x WOF strips to create a 1 ½" x 50 ½" border strip. Repeat to make a total of two strips. Referring to the quilt assembly diagram, sew the two strips to the top and bottom of the quilt top.

6. Sandwich the quilt top, batting, and backing; baste. Quilt as desired, then bind. Tammy custom-quilted a double-echo pattern around the appliqué shapes, then filled in the background with circles. A whimsical design was quilted in the borders.

QUILT ASSEMBLY DIAGRAM

# Laurel

Hand appliquéd and machine pieced by Dawn Heese
Machine quilted by Tammy Bush of
Form and Function Custom Quilting

*The classic wreath design* was a popular choice for 19th-century quilters, who incorporated them into sampler quilts as well as spotlighted them in an entire quilt. Often the same wreath design was repeated for each block. Wrought in red and green fabrics, wreath quilts were often reserved for special guests and made for special occasions, such as weddings. You might think that the wide red sashing with cream vines is the modern twist in my quilt, but that is actually a design element from an 1840s quilt. The modern element is the touches of bright turquoise and the nine very different wreath designs. There are so many beautiful 19th-century wreath designs that I chose to honor nine of them rather than repeating just one design. I think that approach makes for a quilt that is more interesting to the eye as well as the maker!

FINISHED QUILT: 70" X 70"
FINISHED BLOCK: 15" X 15"

## Fabric Requirements

○ 3 ½ yards cream print for block background and borders
○ 1 ⅜ yards cream tone-on-tone for stems and leaves
○ 2 ⅛ yards red print for block appliqué, sashing appliqué, and inner border
○ 2" scrap of different red print than above for block 5
○ ⅜ yard blue print for block appliqué and sashing appliqué
○ 2 ⅜ yards total of two green prints for block appliqué and sashing appliqué
○ ¾ yard red print for bias binding

## Cutting Instructions

**From cream print, cut:**
- 9—15 ½" squares. Then seal the edges with Fray Check to prevent raveling and distortion
- 7—6 ½" strips the width of fabric for outer border

**From red print, cut:**
- 6—2" strips the width of fabric for inner border
- 6—5 ½" x 15 ½" strips for sashing. Then seal the edges with Fray Check to prevent raveling and distortion
- 3—5 ½" strips the width of fabric for sashing

**From red print, cream tone-on-tone, blue print, and two different green prints, cut:**
- Templates on pages 71—80 the number of times noted

## APPLIQUÉ BLOCKS

BLOCK 1

To create a placement guide for your wreath stem, use a chalk pencil to mark a circle that measures 8 ½" in diameter. Line the inside edge of the stem along the marked line. Referring to the templates on page 71 and photo at left for placement, appliqué the shapes to the background square. Stems are made using a ¼" bias tape maker.

BLOCK 2

To create a placement guide for your wreath stem, use a chalk pencil to mark a circle that measures 9 ½" in diameter. Line the inside edge of the stem along the marked line. Referring to the templates on page 72 and photo at left for placement, appliqué the shapes to the background square. Stems are made using a ½" bias tape maker.

**BLOCK 3**

To create a placement guide for your wreath stem, use a chalk pencil to mark a circle that measures 10" in diameter. Line the inside edge of the stem along the marked line. Referring to the templates on page 73 and photo at left for placement, appliqué the shapes to the background square. Stems are made using a ½" bias tape maker.

**BLOCK 4**

To create a placement guide for your wreath stem, use a chalk pencil to mark a circle that measures 11" in diameter. Line the inside edge of the stem along the marked line. Referring to the templates on page 74 and photo at left for placement, appliqué the shapes to the background square. Stems are made using a ½" bias tape maker.

BLOCK 5

To create a placement guide for your wreath stem, use a chalk pencil to mark a circle that measures 9" in diameter. Line the inside edge of the stem along the marked line. Referring to the templates on page 75 and photo at left for placement, appliqué the shapes to the background square. Stems are made using a ¼"bias tape maker.

BLOCK 6

To create a placement guide for your wreath stem, use a chalk pencil to mark a circle that measures 10" in diameter. Line the inside edge of the stem along the marked line. Referring to the templates on page 76 and photo at left for placement, appliqué the shapes to the background square. Stems are made using a ¼" bias tape maker.

BLOCK 7

To create a placement guide for your wreath stem, use a chalk pencil to mark a circle that measures 10" in diameter. Line the inside edge of the stem along the marked line. Referring to the templates on page 77 and photo at left for placement, appliqué the shapes to the background square. Stems are made using a ½" bias tape maker.

BLOCK 8

To create a placement guide for your wreath stem, use a chalk pencil to mark a circle that measures 9" in diameter. Line the inside edge of the stem along the marked line. Referring to the templates on page 78 and photo at left for placement, appliqué the shapes to the background square. Stems are made using a ¼" bias tape maker.

To create a placement guide for your wreath stem, use a chalk pencil to mark a circle that measures 10" in diameter. Line the inside edge of the stem along the marked line. Referring to the templates on page 79 and photo at left for placement, appliqué the shapes to the background square. The main stem is made using a ½" bias tape maker and the smaller stems are made using a ¼" bias tape maker.

# SHORT SASHING STRIPS

1.  Seal the edges of the 6—5 ½" x 15 ½" sashing strips with Fray Check to prevent raveling and distortion.

2.  Referring to the following photo for placement, appliqué the shapes to the six sashing strips. The stems are made using ¼" bias tape maker.

# LONG SASHING STRIPS

1.  Join the 5 ½" x WOF strips, then cut to measure 5 ½" x 55 ½". Make a total of 2—5 ½" x 55 ½" sashing strips.

2.  Seal the edges of the 2—5 ½" x 55 ½" sashing strips with Fray Check to prevent raveling and distortion.

3.  Referring to the photo to the right for placement, appliqué the shapes to the sashing strip. The stems are made using a ¼" bias tape maker.

1. Referring to the diagram below, sew the nine appliquéd blocks and six appliquéd
   5 ½" x 15 ½" sashing strips into three vertical rows. Each vertical row should have
   three appliquéd blocks and two appliquéd sashing strips.

2. Referring to the quilt assembly diagram on page 63, join the three vertical rows from
   step 1 with the two appliquéd 5 ½" x 55 ½" sashing strips to complete the quilt center.

## INNER BORDER

1. Join the red 2" x WOF strips, then cut to measure 2" x 55 ½". Repeat to make a total of two border strips. Referring to the quilt assembly diagram on page 63, sew the two strips to the sides of the quilt center.

2. Join the remaining red 2" x WOF strips, then cut to measure 2" x 58 ½". Repeat to make a total of two border strips. Referring to the quilt assembly diagram, sew the two strips to the top and bottom of the quilt center.

## OUTER BORDER

1. Join the cream print 6 ½" x WOF strips, then cut to measure 6 ½" x 58 ½". Repeat to make a total of two border strips. Referring to the quilt assembly diagram, sew the two strips to the sides of the quilt top.

2. Join the remaining cream print 6 ½" x WOF strips, then cut to measure 6 ½" x 70 ½". Repeat to make a total of two border strips. Referring to the quilt assembly diagram, sew the two strips to the top and bottom of the quilt top.

3. Sandwich the quilt top, batting, and backing; baste. Quilt as desired but do NOT yet bind. Tammy quilted feathers behind all the wreaths and in the outer border. The red borders and sashing are quilted with a small floral design around the appliqué.

QUILT ASSEMBLY DIAGRAM

## CREATING THE SCALLOPS

1. The quilt should be quilted before you make your
   scallops. Then trace the scallop templates on page 80
   onto freezer paper and cut on the traced line.

2. Using a chalk pencil, mark the scallops on all sides
   of the front of the quilt. Do NOT cut on the marked
   line as it is the sewing line.

## BINDING

1. Since the border of this quilt is scalloped, you must
   use bias binding strips, which make it easy to follow
   the curves of the quilt (See page 10 for instructions
   on making bias binding).

2. Starting on the rounded part of the scallop, sew the
   bias binding on the marked line, using a ¼" seam
   allowance and aligning the raw edges of the binding
   with the marked line.

3. Stitch to the base of the valley between the scallops.
   Stop with the needle down, pivot, then sew out of
   the valley. Be careful to avoid creating pleats.

4. Once the binding has been sewn in place, carefully
   cut away the excess border.

5. Turn the binding over to the back of the quilt and
   hand-stitch it in place.

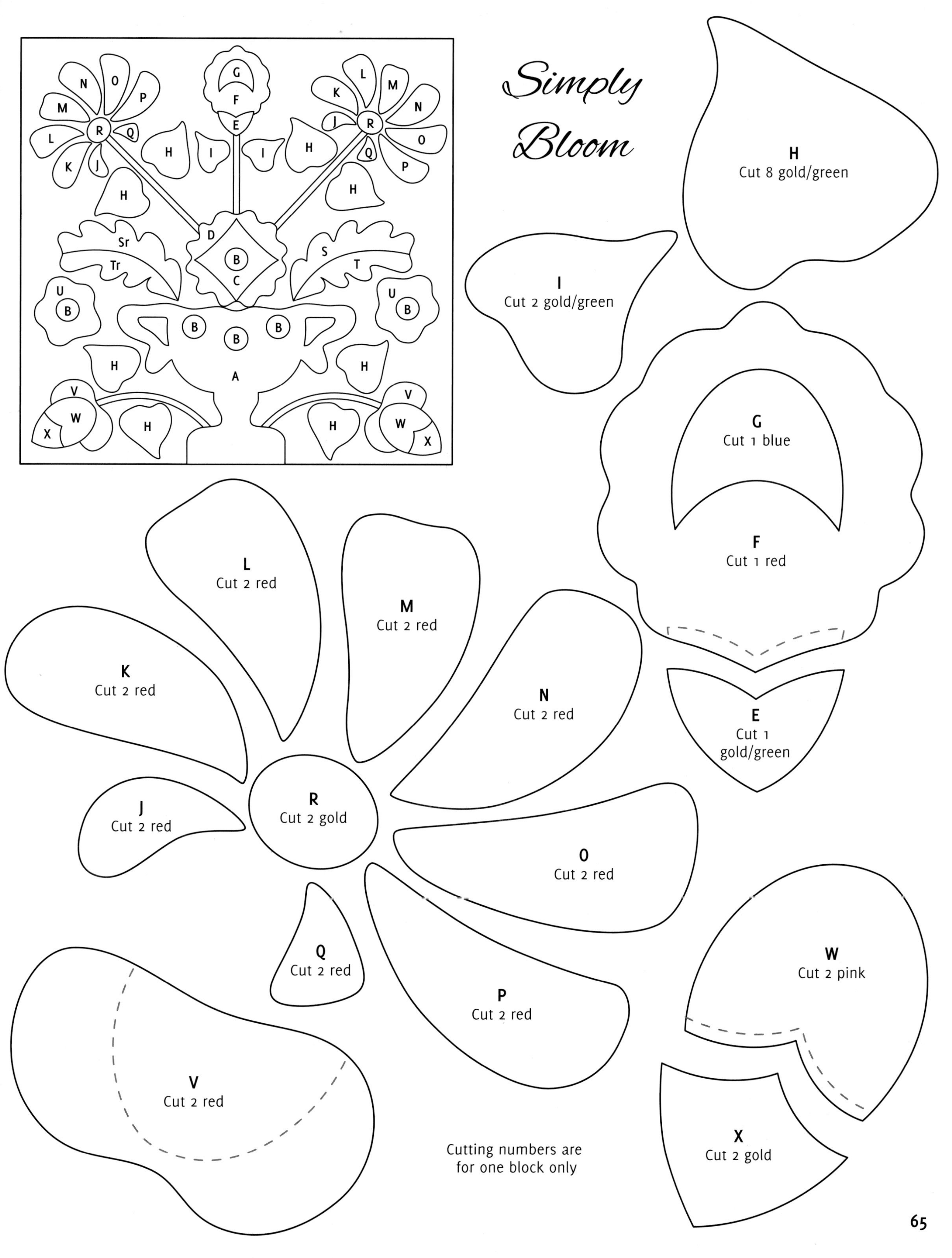


Simply Bloom

H
Cut 8 gold/green

I
Cut 2 gold/green

G
Cut 1 blue

F
Cut 1 red

E
Cut 1 gold/green

L
Cut 2 red

M
Cut 2 red

K
Cut 2 red

N
Cut 2 red

J
Cut 2 red

R
Cut 2 gold

O
Cut 2 red

Q
Cut 2 red

P
Cut 2 red

W
Cut 2 pink

X
Cut 2 gold

V
Cut 2 red

Cutting numbers are
for one block only

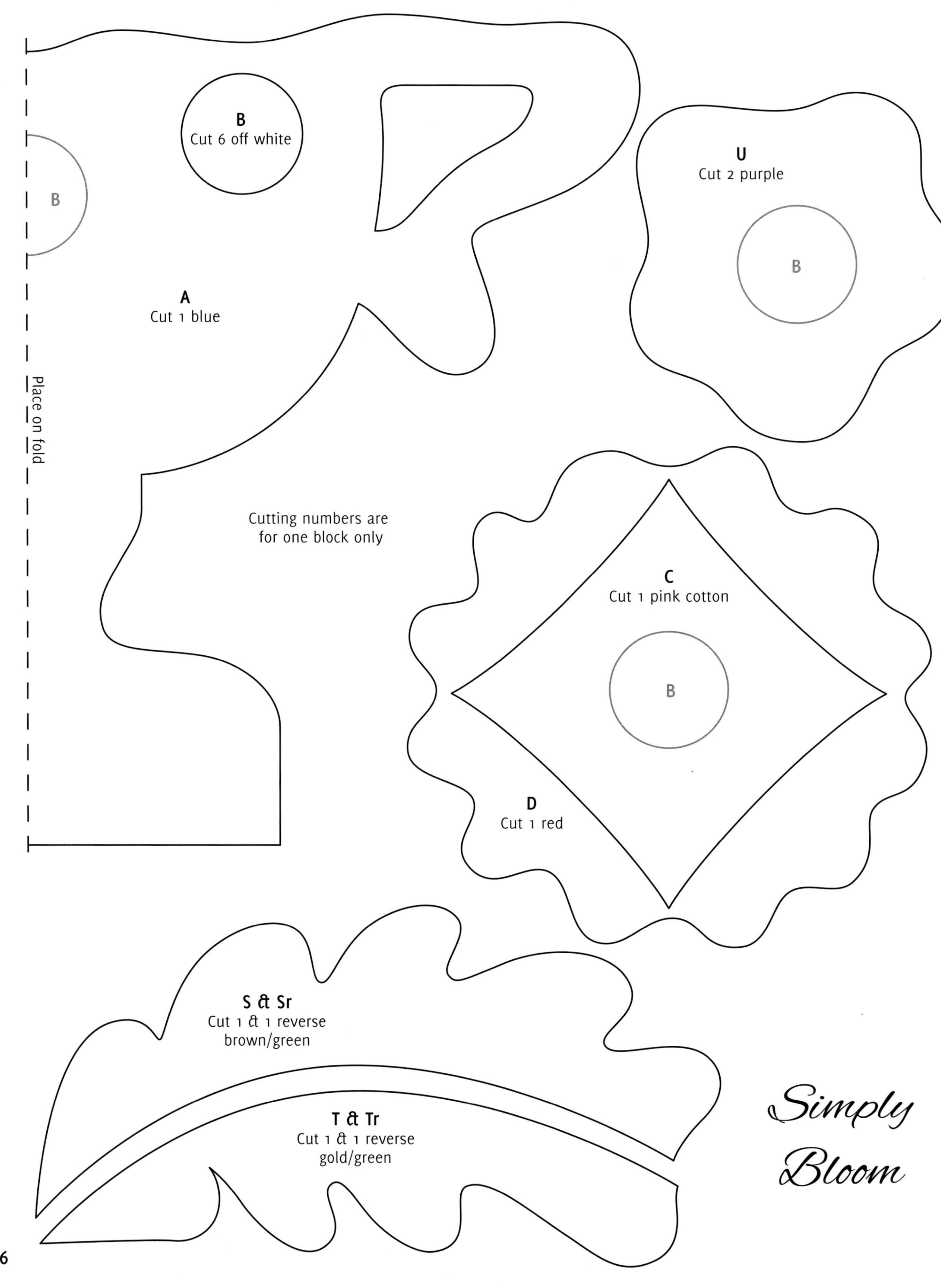

B
Cut 6 off white

B

U
Cut 2 purple

B

A
Cut 1 blue

Place on fold

Cutting numbers are
for one block only

C
Cut 1 pink cotton

B

D
Cut 1 red

S & Sr
Cut 1 & 1 reverse
brown/green

T & Tr
Cut 1 & 1 reverse
gold/green

Simply
Bloom

AA

Z

Simply Bloom

AA
Cut 78 brown/green

AA

Z
Cut 38
off white

Y
Cut 14 red
Cut 14 blue
Cut 10 purple

AA

Y

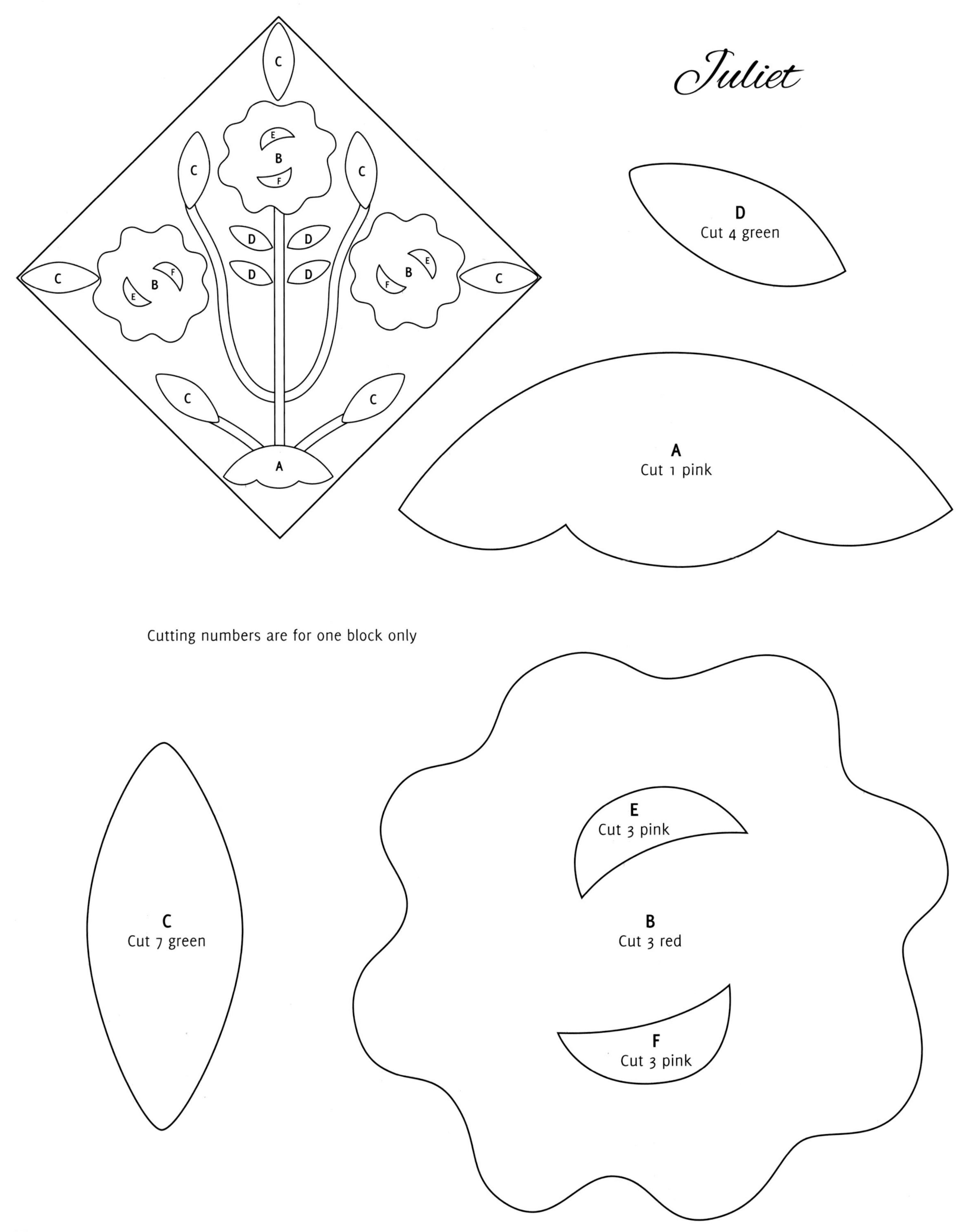

Juliet
C
E
B
F
C
C
C
E
B
F
F
B
E
C
D D
D D
C C
A
D
Cut 4 green
A
Cut 1 pink
Cutting numbers are for one block only
C
Cut 7 green
E
Cut 3 pink
B
Cut 3 red
F
Cut 3 pink

# Hippy Chick

B
B
A
B
Cut 7 orange for throw or 13 for twin size
B
Cut 28 white
for throw
or 52 for
twin size

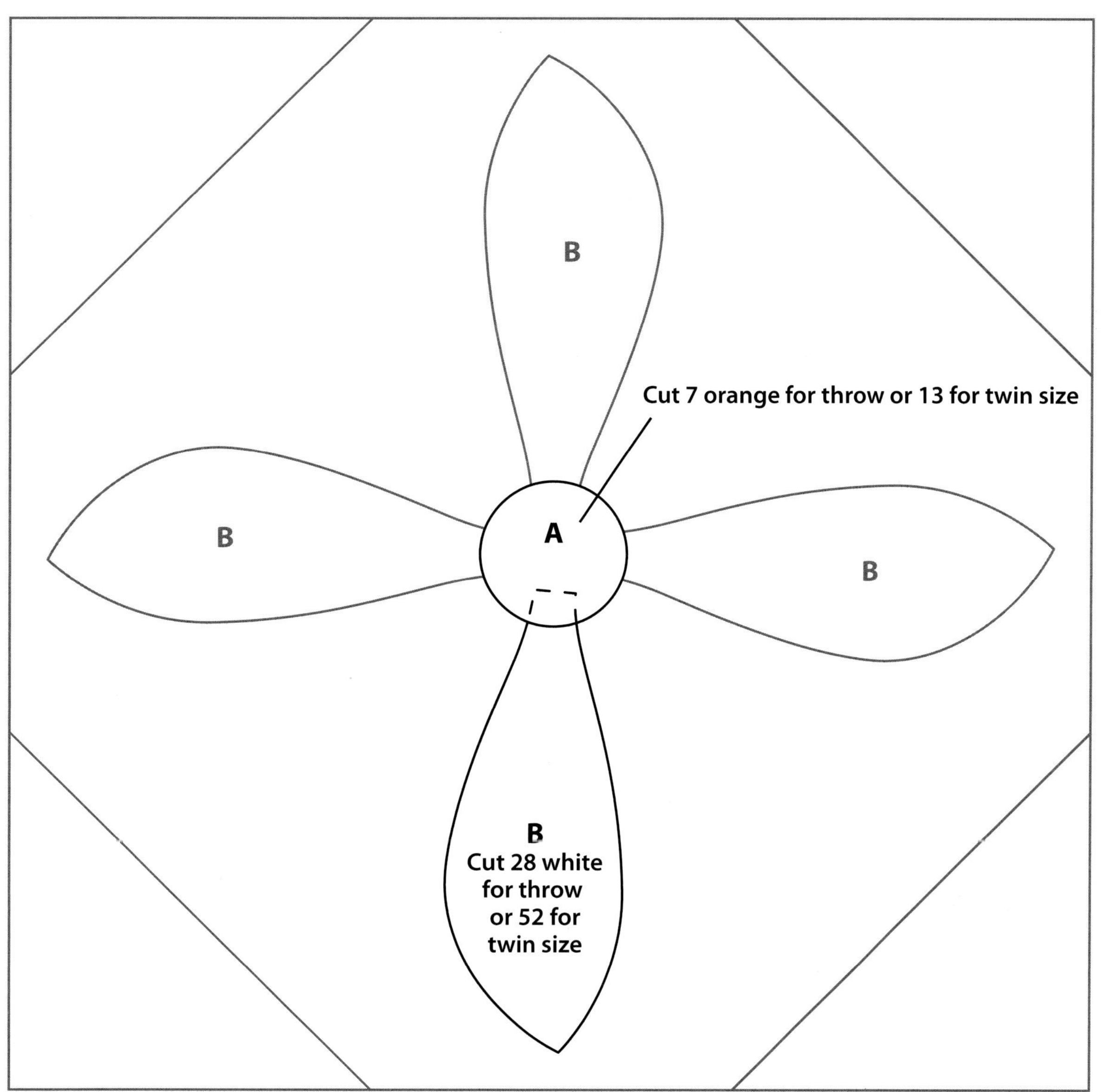

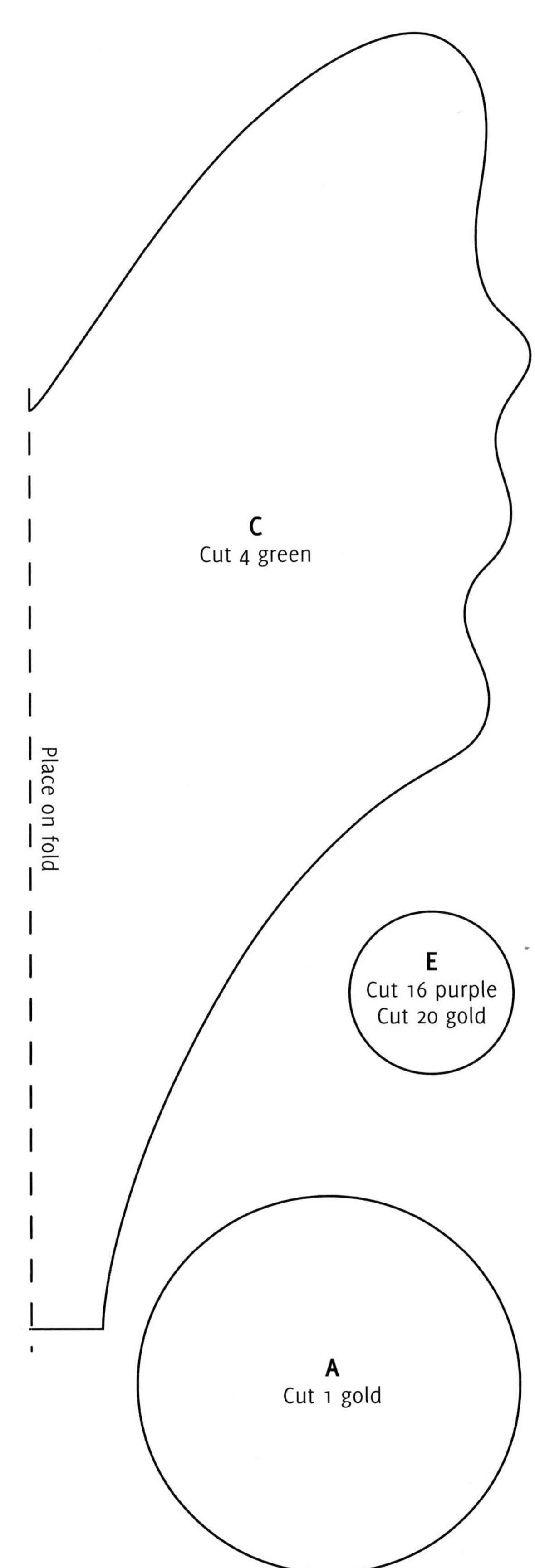

# *Mardi Gras*

**C**
Cut 4 green

Place on fold

**E**
Cut 16 purple
Cut 20 gold

**A**
Cut 1 gold

Cutting numbers are for one block only

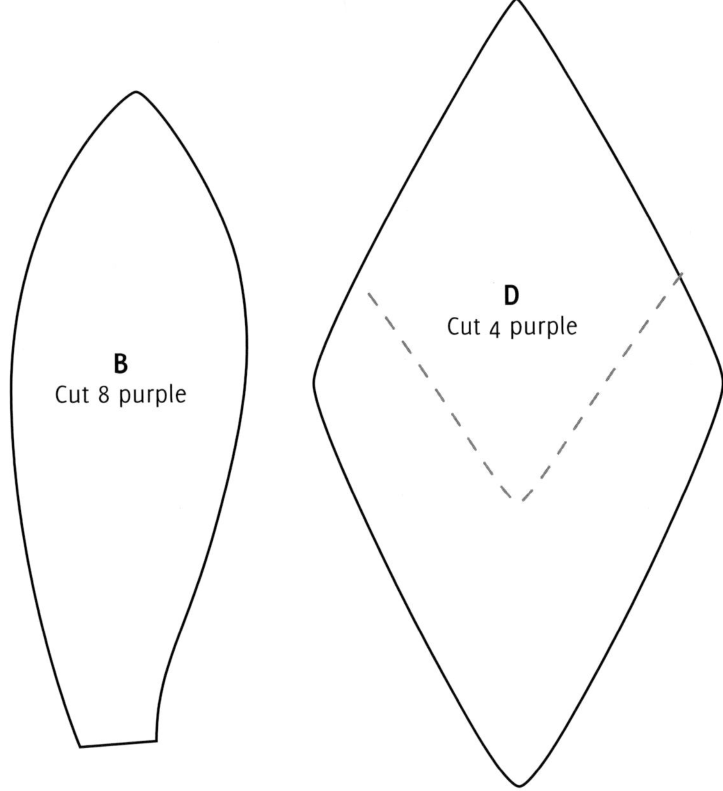

**B**
Cut 8 purple

**D**
Cut 4 purple

70

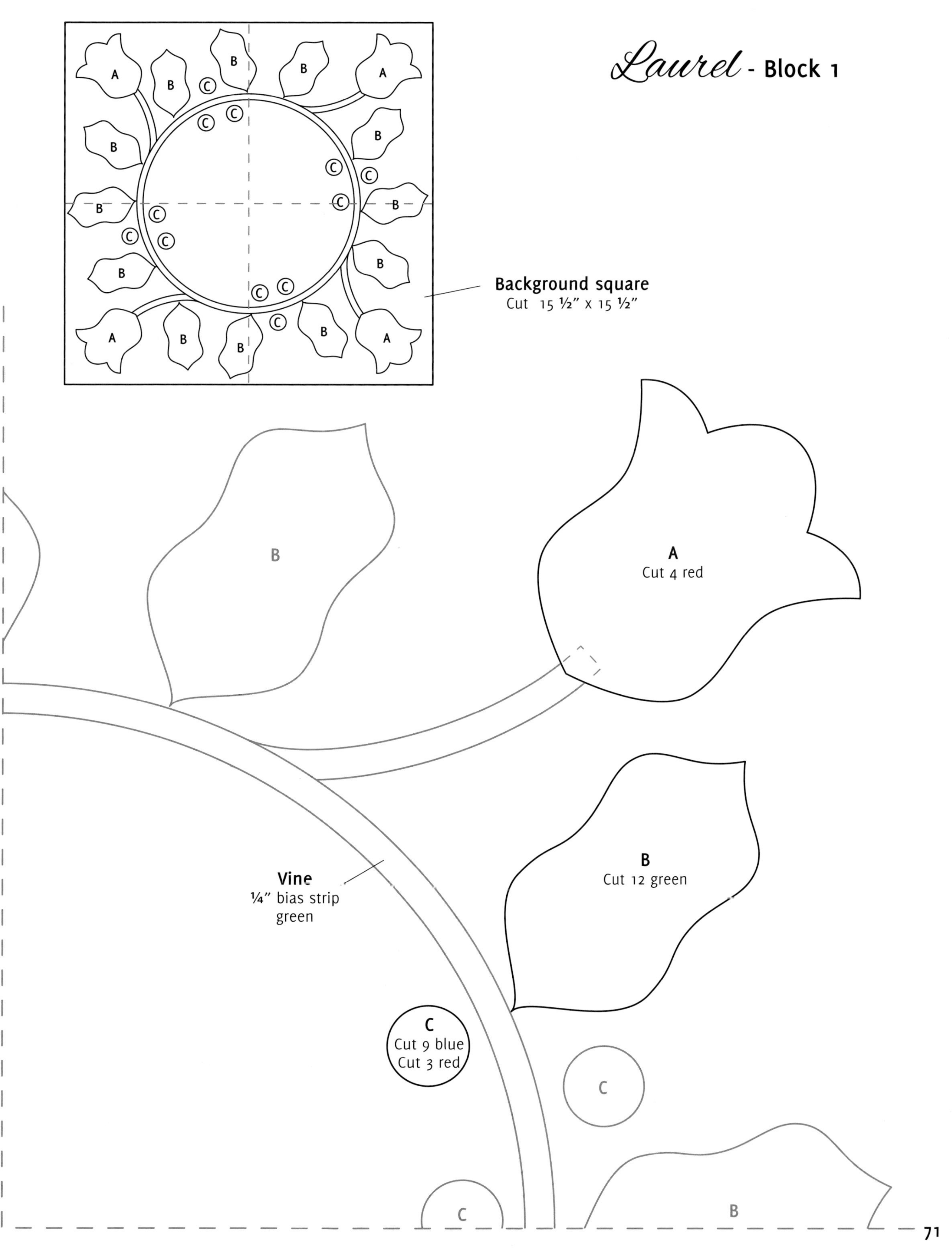


Laurel - Block 1

A

B

B

B

B

B

B

B

A

B

C

C

C

C

C

C

C

C

C

C

B

A

B

B

B

A

Background square
Cut 15 ½" x 15 ½"

B

A
Cut 4 red

B
Cut 12 green

Vine
¼" bias strip
green

C
Cut 9 blue
Cut 3 red

C

C

B

# *Laurel* - **Block 2**

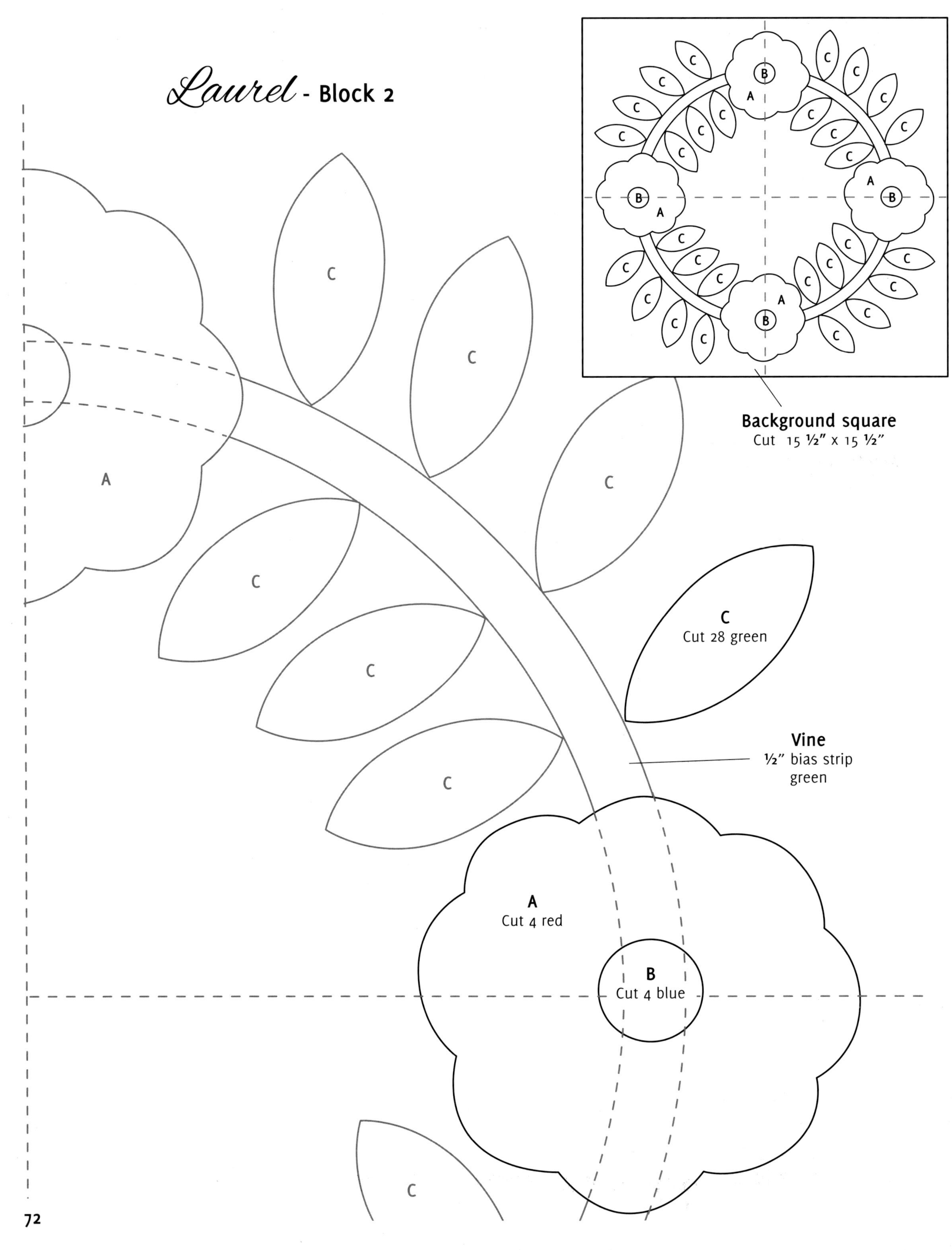

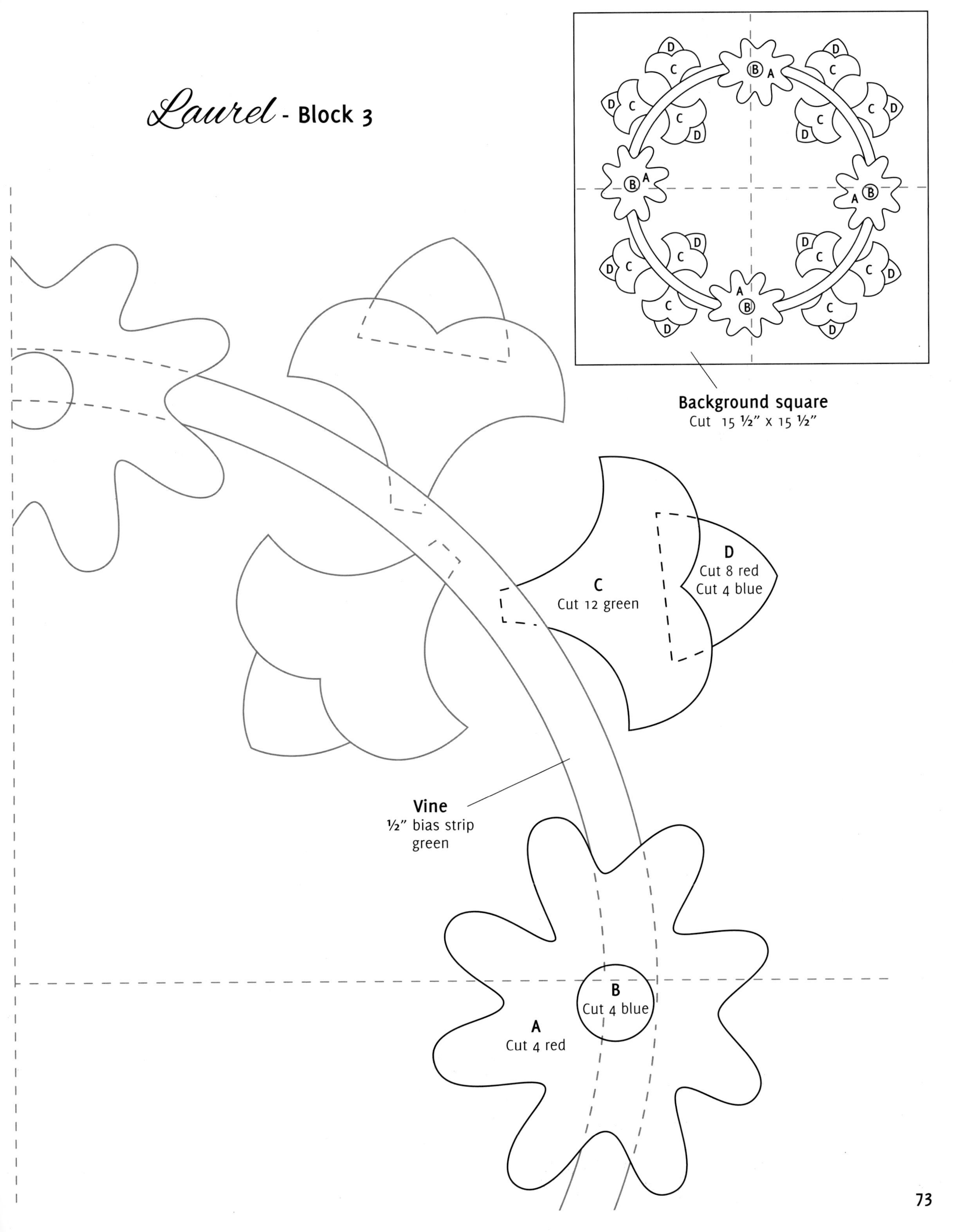


Laurel - Block 3

D
C
B A
C
D

Background square
Cut 15 ½" x 15 ½"

D
Cut 8 red
Cut 4 blue

C
Cut 12 green

Vine
½" bias strip
green

B
Cut 4 blue

A
Cut 4 red

Laurel - Block 4
D
A
Cut 2 red
B
Cut 2 blue
C
Cut 2 red
D
Cut 24 green
D
D
D
D
Background square
Cut 15 ½" x 15 ½"
Vine
½" bias strip
green

Laurel - Block 5

D
Cut 25
green

Background square
Cut 15 ½" x 15 ½"

Vine
¼" bias strip
green

C
Cut 5 blue
Cut 8 green

B
Cut 1 red

A
Cut 1
alternate
red scrap

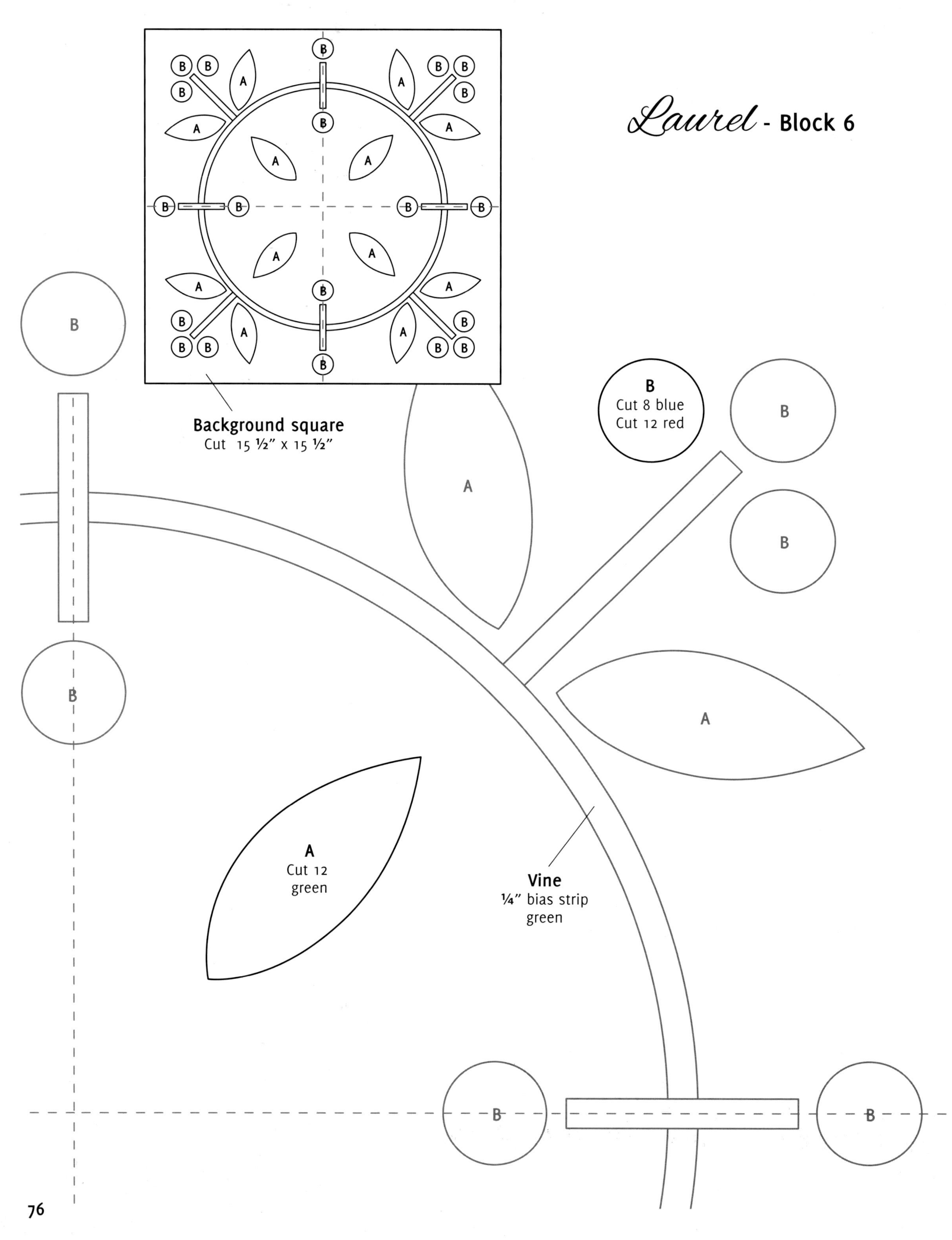

Laurel - Block 6
Background square
Cut 15 ½" x 15 ½"
B
Cut 8 blue
Cut 12 red
A
Cut 12
green
Vine
¼" bias strip
green

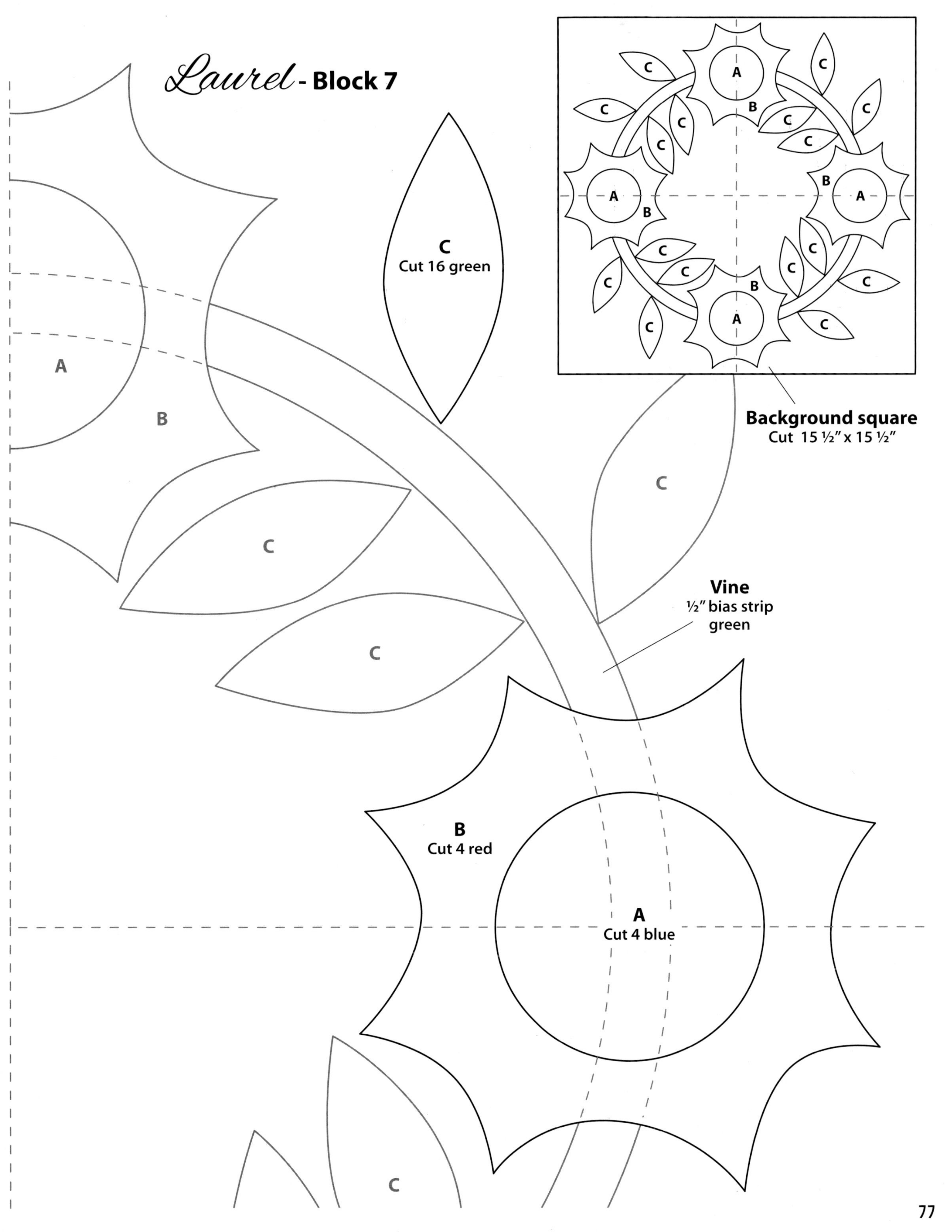

Laurel - Block 7
C
Cut 16 green
A
B
C
C
C
Background square
Cut 15 ½" x 15 ½"
C
Vine
½" bias strip
green
B
Cut 4 red
A
Cut 4 blue
C

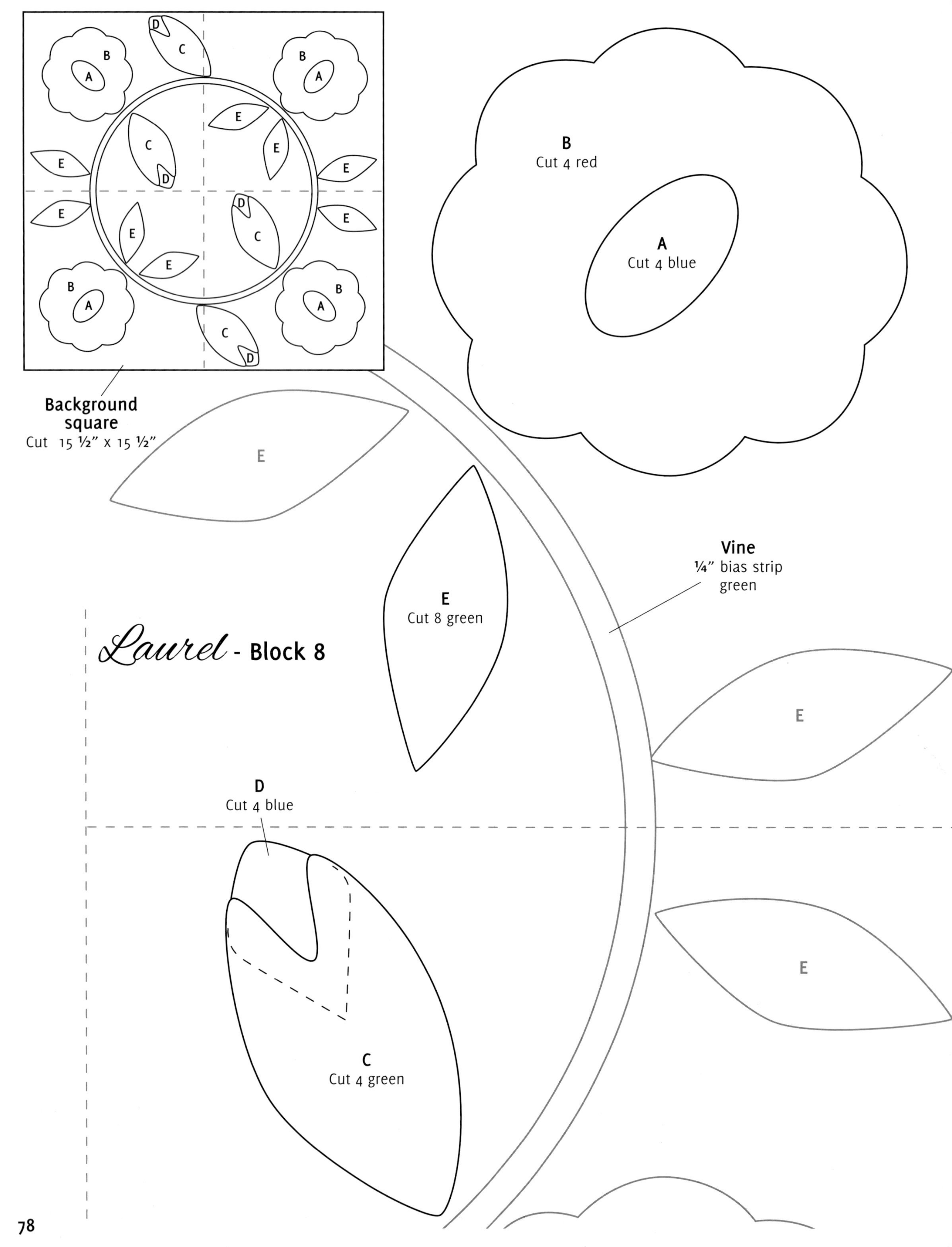


*Laurel* - **Block 8**

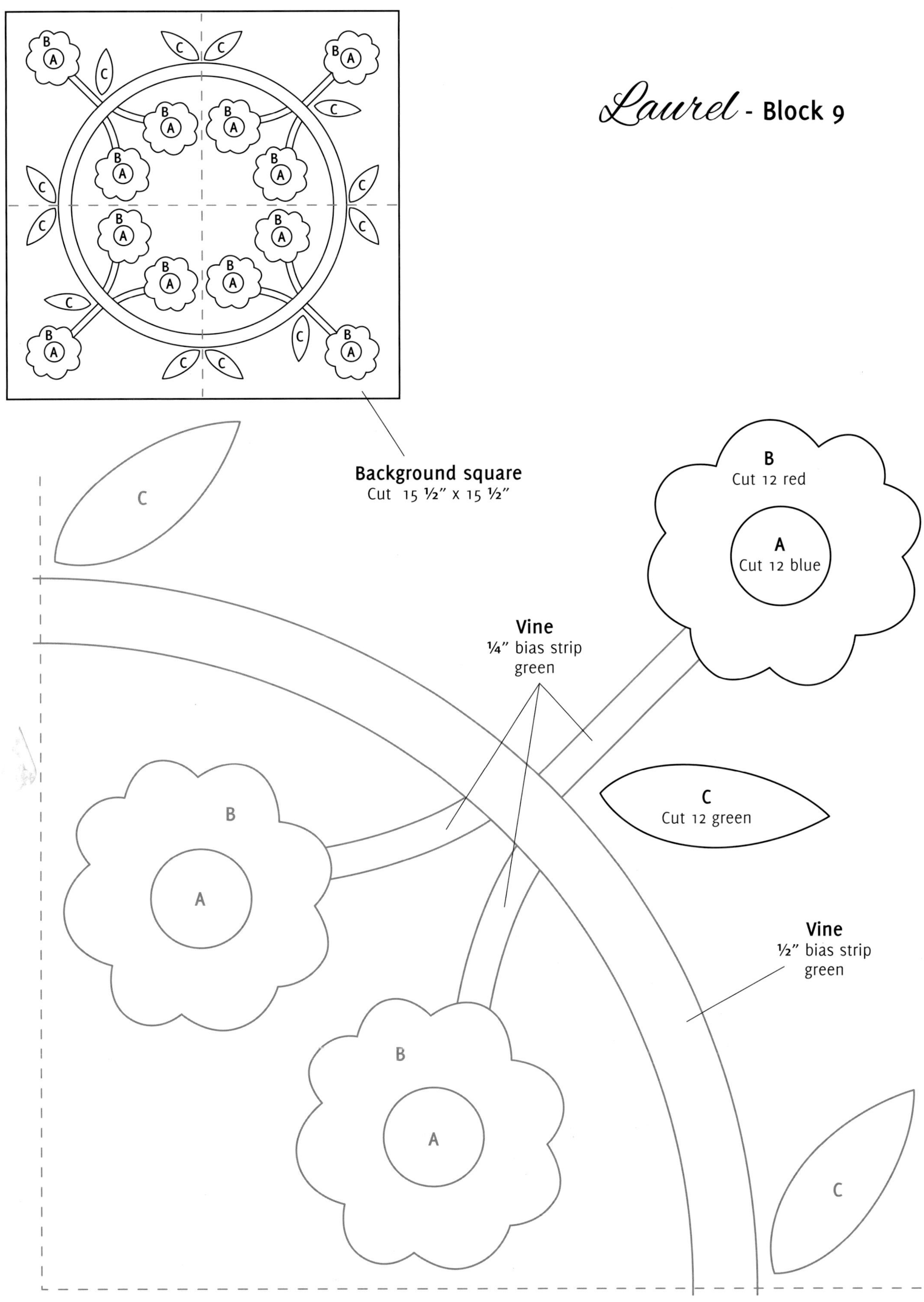



# Laurel - Block 9

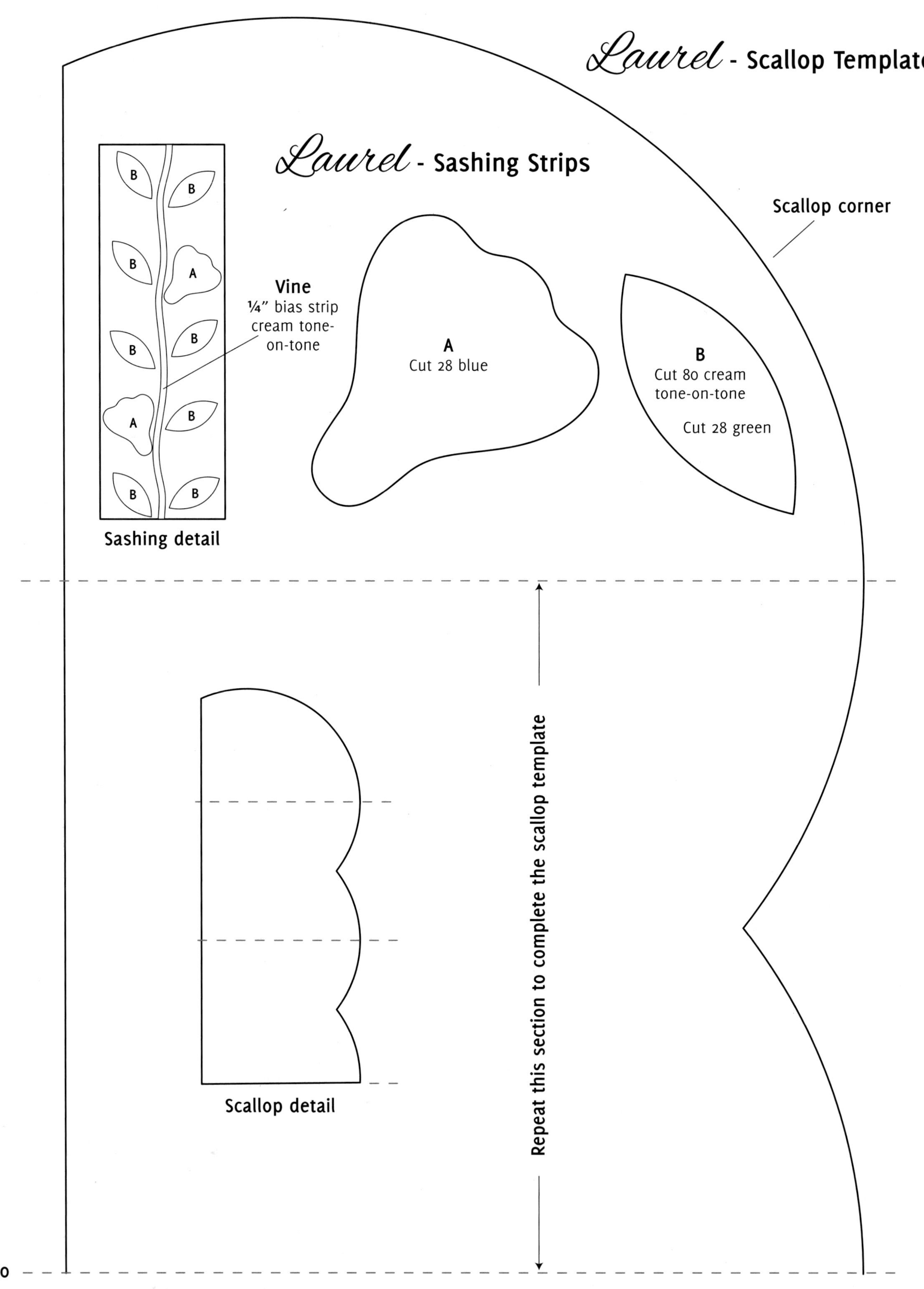
Laurel - Sashing Strips
Scallop corner
B
B
B
A
B
B
B
A
B
B
B
Vine
¼" bias strip cream tone-on-tone
Sashing detail
A
Cut 28 blue
B
Cut 80 cream tone-on-tone
Cut 28 green
Scallop detail
Repeat this section to complete the scallop template